When Friends Cook

Presented by the Friends of The Minneapolis Institute of Arts
1992

Additional copies of **When Friends Cook**
may be obtained by contacting:

Friends of the Institute
The Minneapolis Institute of Arts
2400 3rd Avenue South
Minneapolis, Minnesota 55404
(612) 870–3045

The committee producing this book has taken every
precaution to ensure that all recipes have been tested,
but disclaim responsibility for any error in quantities or
ingredients. We have credited chefs, restaurants and
authors when recipe source information was available.

Cover design by:
Bruce Edwards

Cover photography by:
Graham Brown

Interior photographs courtesy of:

The Minneapolis Institute of Arts
Photo credits: *Pepper No. 30*, by Edward Weston,

© 1981 Arizona Board of Regents, Center for Creative Photography

Printed in the United States by:
Viking Press, Inc., A Banta Corporation Subsidiary
7000 Washington Avenue South
Eden Prairie, Minnesota 55344

Contents

History of the Friends of the Institute

The Friends of the Institute began in January 1922 as a gathering of six friends called together by Mrs. George Christian to remember Ethel Morrison Van Derlip, who had died the previous November. In 1913, Clinton Morrison, Mrs. Van Derlip's father, donated to the Minneapolis Society of Fine Arts "Villa Rosa," the Morrison family estate. In January 1915 the Institute, built on this site, opened its doors to the public. This dedicated group assembled to honor Mrs. Van Derlip's memory and to acknowledge her significant contribution to the Institute. They formed a committee to consult with museum director Russell A. Plimpton and the trustees on how best to carry on her work.

With a sense of urgency, the trustees discussed and approved the general plans and purpose of the fledgling Friends organization the following month. From the beginning, the devotion of this formative group of committed women was evident in the pages of the minutes of their regular meetings. Seventy years later, the Friends, now including men and women, are still dedicated to their original premise of "broadening the influence of the museum in the community."

In its first year of existence, the Friends organized study groups and classes, established a house committee and emphasized the importance of bringing people into the museum. At the Friends annual meeting in 1926, Mr. Plimpton and Society president John Van Derlip outlined plans to complete galleries on the second floor of the new wing. Mrs. Sumner McKnight, first vice president, stated that "the Friends had established a reputation for the prompt accomplishment of whatever they undertook," and she asked the assembled members for subscriptions in $2,000 pledges. The next line read, "The total amount of $24,000 was given by twelve members at the end of twenty minutes."

Raising funds in imaginative ways, in order to enhance their treasured Institute, has always been a raison d'être of the Friends.

- *During the second half of the 1920's and the 1930's, the Friends membership grew and contributed money to furnish the period rooms and to purchase library books and paintings.*

- *"Opportunity sales" were successful fund-raisers during 1940's. Friends collected and sold household goods, objects d'art, glass, china, silver and jewelry from each other's drawers, closets and attics.*

- *Christmas festivals held in the 1950's were the Friends novel gift to the community. Members were invited to set holiday tables, each representing a different country. These picturesque tables were then placed throughout the museum, carols echoed through the galleries and special events took place every day of this three-day event. The day after the 1957 Festival opened, the museum registered the largest single-day crowd to date, 17,565 visitors.*

ᗜ *The first Dayton's Oval Room Fashion Show was held in Dayton's Tea Room in 1952. In the fall of 1991, a forty—year collaboration between a major retail store and the Institute once again brought to Minneapolis internationally acclaimed designers of women's clothing.*

ᗜ *The Museum Shop opened in 1958 to sell art-related gifts, books and objects. In 1991, the Museum Shop, staffed by Friends, contributed $120,116 to The Minneapolis Institute of Arts.*

ᗜ *In 1962 the Friends established a docent program for conducting tours of the museum's collection; Mrs. John Pillsbury, Jr. was its first chairperson. In 1991, 123 docents led 66,560 people on informative walks through the galleries.*

ᗜ *In 1976 the Friends raised funds by offering tours of their first "designer showcase" home, the so-called Pink Palace in Orono. Later the Skinner House in St. Paul and "Green Trees," Mrs. George Halpin's French villa overlooking Lake Minnetonka, were sites of similar fund-raising events.*

ᗜ *The Friends have presented Art in Bloom to the community for nine consecutive years. For this three-day springtime gala, garden clubs and individuals are invited to make floral arrangements that reflect the aesthetics of a painting or sculpture in the Institute's collection. In addition, nationally recognized garden and floral designers give lectures and conduct seminars. This highly successful fund-raiser contributed $70,000 to the Friends' coffers in 1992.*

In 1945 Alfred E. Pillsbury presented the Friends board with a bronze motif of two interlocking rings, ᗜ, the ancient Chinese symbol for eternal friendship. It was agreed that this is an appropriate symbol for the Friends, who work cooperatively and companionably to generate money through projects and programs that ensure future generations enjoyment of the rich cultural heritage of our museum.

Wine & Menus

Wine is to the table what the flower is to the garden, the sun to the orchard and love to the heart of poor men.

—Berjanette

Food & Wine
by Jack Farrell

Food and wine are really almost one because wine, in the real sense of the word, is truly a food. It adds another dimension to fine dining. It seems inconceivable to feast on real Beluga without the joy of an ice cold Brut Champagne to accompany it, or the simple appeal of rhubarb pie without a delightful Sauternes to enjoy along with it.

There are many classical combinations of wine and food that are without precedent. However, there are exceptions, too. There is the old adage: "Red wine with red meat, white wine with white meat." That is a good guideline to use when marrying wines with food; however, let's not forget that Italians regularly drink red wine with fish and the Germans, for the most part, drink white wine with almost everything, including red meats.

Part of the joy of putting wine and food together is to experiment with your own combinations until you find what you like best. It would be fairly monotonous to serve the same dish all the time, and so it is with wine. Drinking the same wines all the time becomes dull and not too much fun.

There are some guidelines to follow with your daily meals that are simple and basic. Perhaps a simple wine such as a California Zinfandel or a Sauvignon Blanc would be in order for everyday consumption. Lighter wines are better in warmer weather. In the summer you might want to try a Beaujolais or a Petite Sirah from California with a barbecued steak. Perhaps a California Zinfandel or a Rhône wine from France would go quite well with that barbecued steak. Winter calls for a heavier, more full–bodied wine. In the winter you might prefer a Cabernet Sauvignon or a Burgundy from France or perhaps a big Bordeaux.

A basic premise to follow is that wines should never overwhelm the food, or vice versa. If you are serving a seafood salad, you would not want to serve a big buttery Puligny Montrachet any more than you would want to serve a Gamay Beaujolais with venison. If you are serving light delicate dishes such as veal or trout, you want a clean, crisp wine to accompany these kinds of dishes. A Mosel from Germany or a Chenin Blanc from California or even light, white Italian wines would be best. On the other hand, a robust dish such as spaghetti or a hearty beef stew calls for a bigger, more vigorous wine such as an Italian Barolo or a California Barbera.

At a dinner party, nothing adds more excitement to the meal than the pleasure of looking at a well decorated table with several wine glasses per person. Serving more than one wine with the meal is interesting and fun. Remember that if you are serving more than one wine, light wines precede heavy wines, young wines precede older wines and the lesser wines should always precede the better wines. This is just common sense as, generally, lighter wines accompany the starter course. For example, if your starter course is going to be scallops, you might want to serve a Meursault or a California Chardonnay. If the entrée is going to be lamb, a St. Julien or a California Cabernet would be in order.

A cheese course, usually served after the salad and before dessert, is the course to show off your best bottle of wine, perhaps an old Burgundy or Bordeaux that you have been saving for a special occasion. Wine and cheese are natural partners and go perfectly with each other. Almost every wine goes with every cheese. Naturally there are pairings of wine and cheese that are most interesting and tried and true, but a good overall rule of thumb is that all wine goes with all cheese.

Sauternes cannot be overlooked as an apéritif. They are far less expensive than Champagne and they are good bargains in the world of wine. You can buy a relatively good Sauternes for around twenty dollars a bottle and one bottle will serve approximately ten people. The French frequently serve foie gras with Sauternes successfully, and in many parts of France, Sauternes is always served ice cold as an apéritif. It can be exquisite and will help enhance your reputation as a good host or hostess.

It is interesting to note that Champagnes go with salty food and foods such as Parmesan cheese, while Zinfandel, a peppery red wine, often tastes good with peppery foods. Sweet wines seem to marry best with fruits such as apricots, rhubarb and berries. Sweet wines do not usually go very well with chocolate.

In this book we have endeavored to list some wine suggestions with different foods. They are simply suggestions and meant only as a guideline. Vintages of wines are constantly changing. Usually the style of the wine maker stays the same for as long as the wine maker is with the vineyard, generally anywhere from five to thirty–five years. Therefore, if a wine is recommended with a dish, very often a substitute for a current vintage will serve you very well rather than trying to seek out the specific vintage recommended.

Wine & Cooking
by Jack Farrell

Wine cooking is one of the oldest of man's culinary discoveries. Somewhere along the line it was discovered that adding a little bit of wine to the pot improved the flavor of food. Wine cooking has followed the cultural ascent of man. We have writers of ancient Rome and Greece telling us wine was used as a seasoning. Mediterranean cooks have always used wine in their cooking. In this country our forefathers spoke of it glowingly. Martha Washington's cookbook contained several recipes using wine. Thomas Jefferson and Ben Franklin used wine in their cooking. Ben Franklin, as a matter of fact, considered himself an expert on the subject of cooking with wine.

Cooking with wine is pretty basic. It is like using any other spice. Use it sparingly. Wine can improve the flavor of almost any dish without overpowering it. It blends well with other flavors of food and will add an extra dimension. Cooking with wine is like cooking with any extract such as vanilla or lemon. The alcohol is cooked away, so all that remains is the flavor of the wine to complement the food.

A helpful hint to remember is to keep a good bottle of dry French vermouth in the kitchen and use it any time a recipe calls for white wine. After all, vermouth is nothing more than white wine with spices added. It will give a delightful taste to any food in the sauté pan.

Remember that wine, because of its natural enzymes, is a tenderizer. It can be used in any beef or game marinade and will help to not only add flavor, but will tenderize the meat as well. Put a little salad oil on the top. The oil on the top will prevent the wine from aerating and oxidizing and becoming like vinegar. Certainly the little bit of oil that is going to cover the top of a bottle of isn't going to spoil any dish.

Wines sold as "cooking wines" should generally be avoided. After all, if a wine isn't fit to drink, it certainly isn't fit to use in cooking.

If you have extra wine, why not make vinegar? This can be easily accomplished by covering the top of the wine bottle with a cheese cloth, adding a little salt to the wine and mixing it half and half with cider vinegar. After that, just add wine as you have surplus, periodically putting in a little cider vinegar to make sure it is quite tasty.

Cooking with wine is a simple endeavor and never should be considered complex or difficult.

Wine improves with age, I like it more the older I get.

—*Jack Farrell*

CHRISTMAS DINNER FOR FRIENDS

Crudités with Roasted Pepper Dip*

Shrimp in Garlic with Shallot Sauce*
Centenaire Brut N/V

Oyster Loaves*
Chateau Maligny Chablis 1990

Crown Roast of Pork*
with Sherried Peach Stuffing*

Ramekins of Cranberry Mousse*

Rutabaga and Turnip Purée*

Hearts of Palm and Pomegranate*
with Raspberry Vinaigrette*
1989 Cotes des Nuits (Faiveley)

Caramelized Flan with Raspberries*
Chateau Latour Blanche 1983

* indicates that recipe is in this book.
Please refer to index.

La Cucina Italiana

Minestrone with Pesto Sauce*

Lemon Roasted Chicken with Rosemary*
Santa Christina (Antinori) 1989

Tuscan–Style Sautéed White Beans*

Braised Spinach and Shallots*

Biscuit Tortoni*

Autumn Luncheon

Positively Pumpkin Soup*
with Cheese Straws

Grilled Chicken Salad*
Frog's Leap Sauvignon Blanc 1991

Cranberry Yogurt Muffins*

Lemon Sherbet and Ginger Lace Cookies*

Mexican Fiesta

Cadillac Bar's Ramos Gin Fizz*

Roy's Picco de Gallo*

Sopa de Tortilla*

Chicken–Green Chile Enchiladas*
Beer: Corona or Dos Equis

Salpicon*
Wine: Torres Viña Sol 1991

Josefinas*

Amaretto Freeze*

Spring Luncheon

Spinach and Fruit Salad*
Fetzer Sundial Chardonnay 1991

Asparagus wrapped in Prosciutto
with melted fontina cheese

Parmesan Puffs*

Old Fashioned Lemon Sponge Dessert*

Landlocked Shore Dinner

Oysters on Half Shell
served on a bed of ice with horseradish cocktail sauce
Cuvée Catherine Muscat Sur Lie 1991

Steamed Grilled Clams

Tuna Steaks with Rosemary Butter*
Kalin Chardonnay 1990

Vegetable Array*

Cold Sliced Tomatoes with Mozzarella Cheese*

Grilled Peaches with Blueberry Sauce*

Spring Picnic

Cold Watercress Soup*

Oven–Fried Chicken*
White: Piesporter Michelsberg 1991

Mushroom Pie*
Red: Duboeuf Beaujolais–Villages 1991

Selection of Cheeses and Fresh Fruit

AN ELEGANT EVENING

Cran–Raspberry Chutney on Brie*
with French Bread Rounds

Belgian Endive Hors d'Oeuvre*

Mushroom Roll* with Hollandaise
Stone Creek Chardonnay 1990

Loin Lamb Chops with Red Pepper and Mint Salsa*

Sugar Snap Peas Stir Fry*

Party Potatoes*

Greens with Basil Vinaigrette*
with Goat Cheese Croutons*
Chateau Greysac 1989

Pears with Champagne
Korbel Brut N/V

Vincent van Gogh

Olive Trees, 1889

The William Hood Dunwoody Fund

PAUL REVERE
Templeman Tea Service, 1792–93
Gift of James F. and Louise H. Bell

MODELED BY JOHANN JOACHIM KÄNDLER
MANUFACTURED BY MEISSEN, from the Swan Service
Pair of Plates, German, 1737–40
The Christina N. and Swan J. Turnblad Memorial Fund

EDOUARD VUILLARD
La Cuisinière, 1899
Gift of Bruce B. Dayton

Appetizers &
First Courses

Small cheer and great welcome makes a merry feast.

—Shakespeare

Caponata (Italian Eggplant)

Can be frozen, but must be reheated or it will be mushy.

⅓	cup olive oil
⅓	cup green pepper, chopped
1	medium onion, chopped
¾	cup mushrooms, sliced
2	garlic cloves, mashed
3	cups eggplant, peeled and chopped
1	6–ounce can tomato paste
¼	cup water
2	tablespoons wine vinegar
½	cup stuffed green olives, coarsely chopped
1½	teaspoons sugar
½	teaspoon oregano
1	teaspoon salt
⅛	teaspoon pepper

Put oil in a large pot. Add next 5 ingredients, the eggplant last, so that it won't absorb all the oil. Cover and cook for 10 minutes.

Add all other ingredients. Mix well. Cover and simmer gently for about 30 minutes.

Serve hot or cold.

Baked New Potatoes with Herbed Yogurt

2-3	new potatoes per person, baked
1	cup low–fat yogurt
2	teaspoons Maggie seasoning
½	cup parsley, chopped
½	cup other herbs, fresh and chopped, or 2 tablespoons dried herbs
1	scant teaspoon Parmesan cheese per potato

Bake potatoes, cool and cut a cross in top of each one. Punch down and place on ovenproof platter.

Mix remaining ingredients except cheese. Place a dollop on each potato and top with cheese.

Heat in 350° oven for 20 minutes and finish by broiling until brown and crunchy.

Mushroom Crab Mornay

Serves 4

1	pound mushrooms, stems removed
2	cups crab meat, flaked
2	teaspoons lemon juice

Sauce:

3	tablespoons butter
3	tablespoons flour
1½	cups milk, whole or 2%
2	egg yolks
1½	cups sharp Cheddar cheese, shredded
2	tablespoons dry sherry
¼	teaspoon salt
¼	teaspoon white pepper

Combine mushrooms, crab and lemon juice in an 8 x 8–inch dish.

Melt butter in saucepan. Add flour slowly, mixing well. Add milk slowly and stir. Add a little of the sauce to slightly beaten egg yolks. Return the egg mixture to the sauce gradually. Add the cheese and sherry.

Pour sauce over the crab meat and mushrooms. Bake at 350° for 20 minutes. Serve over rice or toast points.

Stromboli Antipasto

Serves 8 to 10 as an appetizer or luncheon salad.

4	medium potatoes, skinned, boiled and sliced
1	can water packed tuna, drained
¼	pound mild Italian cheese, such as Bel Paese or Mozzarella, cubed
¼	pound hard Italian salami, cubed
¼	pound thick sliced mortadella, cubed
1	cup olives, black and green
½	cup red onion, blanched and sliced
2	tablespoons capers
1	6–ounce jar marinated artichoke hearts, drained and halved
4	cloves garlic, minced
1	tablespoon oregano, dried
2	tablespoons fresh basil, chopped
1	cup olive oil

Mix together all ingredients and refrigerate for 8 hours.

Serve cool or at room temperature.

Eggplant Sandwiches

Serves 4

4	rounds peeled eggplant, 1 inch thick
	salt and pepper
4	rounds Gorgonzola or Fontina cheese
4	tomato slices
½	cup flour
1	egg, lightly beaten
2	tablespoons water
1	cup fine bread crumbs
	oil for frying

Salt eggplant rounds and drain after 10 minutes. Place each round on flat surface. Slice through middle horizontally with sharp knife, leaving a hinge on each round. Sprinkle with pepper.

Fill each round with slice of cheese and tomato. Close sandwich. Dip each round in flour. Shake off excess.

Combine egg and water. Dredge sides and tops of slices in egg and water mixture. Then dredge in bread crumbs to coat. Shake off excess.

Fill heavy skillet with oil to ½ inch. Heat to 375°. Add sandwiches in one layer and cook, turning occasionally, for 4 to 5 minutes. When golden, drain on paper towels and serve with or without tomato sauce.

Tomato Sauce for Eggplant Sandwiches

Serves 4

Yields 2 cups

3	tablespoons olive oil
1	tablespoon garlic, minced
2	cups canned crushed tomatoes
1	teaspoon oregano, crushed
1	teaspoon rosemary, crushed
	salt and pepper
2	tablespoons fresh basil, chopped

Heat oil in saucepan. Add garlic and cook briefly.

Add tomatoes, oregano, rosemary, salt and pepper. Bring to a boil and cook 15 to 20 minutes, stirring occasionally. Stir in basil leaves.

Miniature Reubens

Yields 30 pieces.

Freezes beautifully.

8	ounces pastrami or corned beef, sliced
1	8–ounce can sauerkraut, drained
¾	cup Thousand Island dressing
1	tablespoon onion, finely chopped
30	slices party rye or 8 ounces rye bread, thinly sliced
8	ounces Swiss cheese

To make with food processor: Place first 4 ingredients into bowl and use metal blade. Turn on and off until shredded enough to spread easily, but not a paste. Make one recipe at a time.

To make with blender: Do half recipe at a time. Cut across meat a few times and through sauerkraut as well. Add remaining ingredients and blend until of spreading consistency.

Spread mixture on bread. Top with slice of Swiss cheese to fit. Broil until cheese has melted.

May be cut in half for 60 bite-size servings.

Marinated Chèvre

Serves 8 to 10

½	inch slices of chèvre, domestic goat cheese, enough to cover bottom of a 10–inch round ceramic dish (flan, tart, or quiche)
½-⅔	cup olive oil
2	garlic cloves, chopped
½	cup sun dried tomatoes packed in olive oil, drained and chopped
½	cup fresh basil, chopped
	large croutons or thinly sliced French bread

Place cheese slices in ceramic dish. Cover cheese with olive oil and sprinkle with garlic. Marinate, covered, in refrigerator for 24 hours.

Remove from refrigerator and sprinkle with the tomatoes and basil. Cover again and allow the cheese to reach room temperature.

Serve with the croutons or French bread. May also be served as a first course.

Salé au Fromage

Serves 5 to 6

Delicious, but rich!

1	9–inch pie shell, unbaked
	flour
12	ounces Gruyère cheese, freshly grated
3	eggs, slightly beaten
12	ounces plain yogurt
3½	ounces cream
	pepper to taste
	paprika

Preheat oven to 375°.

Pierce pie shell and dust with flour. Mix remaining ingredients and pour into pie shell.

Bake until golden, about 25 minutes.

May be served as a first course or a luncheon entrée with a green salad.

Shrimp in Garlic with Shallot Sauce

Serves 8

3	garlic cloves, minced
2	tablespoons olive oil
2	tablespoons butter
½	cup dry white wine
1½	pounds green shrimp

Sauté garlic in oil until golden. Add butter and wine. Simmer over low heat. Add shrimp. Cook until shrimp are no longer opaque.

Remove shrimp with slotted spoon. Reserve drippings for Shallot Sauce.

Shallot Sauce:

½	cup shallots, chopped
3	tablespoons butter
	drippings from shrimp sauté
½	cup heavy cream

Lightly sauté shallots in butter until they are wilted. Add drippings and cream. Simmer until reduced by one–fourth.

Remove from heat. Pour over shrimp on warm platter.

Oyster Loaves

Serves 8

8	brioche or dinner rolls
24	large oysters, shucked
¼	cup melted butter
2	tablespoons unsalted butter
2	teaspoons flour
½	cup heavy cream
	white pepper

Slice off top quarter of brioche or rolls. Scoop out most of the inside. Brush inside of rolls with melted butter. Replace top.

Bake at 350° for 8 minutes.

Sieve oysters for impurities and set aside in their own liquor.

In a saucepan, melt butter and whisk in flour. Cook 2 minutes. Add cream and some oyster liquor. Add oysters and bring to boil. Immediately remove oysters from sauce with slotted spoon. Put 3 oysters into each brioche. Pour remaining sauce into each one. Replace top.

Heat in oven for 5 to 10 minutes.

Baked Oysters or Clams in Tarragon Butter

24	oysters or cherrystone clams, opened
4	tablespoons tarragon-Pernod butter
	rock salt

Preheat oven to 500° for 30 minutes.

Place oysters or clams on baking sheet on 1–inch of rock salt. Place ½ teaspoon of Tarragon Butter on each oyster or clam. Bake 3 to 5 minutes.

Tarragon–Pernod Butter:

1½	tablespoons fresh tarragon
	or
2	teaspoons dried tarragon
1½	teaspoons tarragon vinegar
1	teaspoon Pernod
½	teaspoon pepper
8	tablespoons butter, cut into pieces

Place all ingredients in food processor. Blend well.

Makes 4 tablespoons.

Mushroom Roll

Serves 6 to 8

Good hot or cold.

	oil
1½	pounds mushrooms, chopped
6	eggs, separated
¼	pound butter, melted
½	teaspoon salt
¼	teaspoon pepper
2	tablespoons lemon juice
4-5	whole mushrooms, fluted
	butter
	lemon juice
	salt and pepper
	parsley, chopped
	hollandaise or hot butter

Oil a jelly roll pan. Line with waxed paper. Oil paper.

Chop cleaned mushrooms in food processor. Squeeze mushrooms in cloth to remove moisture. Beat egg yolks and combine with mushrooms, butter, salt, pepper and lemon juice.

Beat egg whites to soft peaks and fold into mushroom mixture. Spread gently over oiled paper in pan. Bake for 15 minutes at 350°. Cool. Turn out onto sheet of waxed paper and peel off paper. Roll up and place on platter.

Sauté fluted mushrooms in butter over high heat for 2 minutes.

Sprinkle with lemon juice, salt and pepper. Arrange mushrooms on top of roll.

Sprinkle with parsley and serve with hot butter or hollandaise.

May be prepared in advance and reheated.

Onion Puffs

Yields 25 to 30 pieces

1	cup mayonnaise, not low calorie
½	package Lipton onion soup mix
1	package thin Norwegian flat bread
	Parmesan cheese

Mix mayonnaise and onion soup mix. Spread on pieces of flat bread. Lay them out on an ungreased cookie sheet. Sprinkle with Parmesan cheese.

Bake at 350° about 8 to 10 minutes, watching carefully. Remove when cheese is bubbly.

Fresh Asparagus Rolls

Yields 32 to 40 pieces

8	slices white or multi-grained bread, crusts removed
2	tablespoons melted butter
8	asparagus stalks, bases snapped off
½	cup melted black currant jam
	endive
	Parmesan cheese, freshly grated

Preheat broiler to 400°.

Roll bread slices until flat. Brush both sides of each piece with melted butter.

Cook asparagus in lightly salted boiling water just until tender. Drain and rinse in cold water to retain color. Place individually on drainer to allow all water to drain off.

Brush one side of each bread slice with jam. Place asparagus spear on one edge of jam coated bread slice and roll bread to enclose spear. Cut off blunt end of spear even with bread. Place on non-stick or oiled baking sheet. Broil for approximately 4 minutes, then turn and broil for 3 or 4 more minutes.

Serve as an hors d'oeuvre by cutting each roll into 4 to 5 pieces, turning up each piece to reveal asparagus.

Serve as first course by putting two rolls on each plate atop a bed of curly endive. Sprinkle rolls and endive with freshly grated Parmesan cheese.

Vidalia Onion Spread

2	Vidalia onions, thinly sliced
1	cup water
¼	cup white vinegar
¼	cup sugar
	mayonnaise
	Ritz crackers

Marinate onions in water, vinegar and sugar for 3 to 4 hours. Drain and pat dry.

Finely chop onions and mix with mayonnaise. Serve on Ritz crackers.

To extend the life of Vidalia onions, store them in pantyhose making a twist between each onion. Hang them up in a dark closet.

Lima Bean Teasers

Yields 24 pieces

1	package frozen baby Lima beans
8	ounces sour cream
¾	cup Parmesan cheese, divided
24	croustades, ready–to–use version in grocery freezer section

Preheat broiler to 425°.

Cook Lima beans in lightly salted water until just tender. Drain and run under cold water. Drain again and hold.

Mix sour cream with ½ cup of Parmesan. Place a tablespoon in each croustade. Add 5 Lima beans to each croustade, taking time to arrange in an orderly circle. Sprinkle with remaining Parmesan cheese.

Broil 4 to 5 minutes or until bubbly and golden brown on top. Serve warm.

Ham Balls

Yields approximately 11 dozen

Ham Balls:

1	pound ground ham
1	pound ground pork sausage
2	cups soft bread crumbs
1	cup milk

Sauce:

1	cup brown sugar
1	teaspoon dry mustard
½	cup water
½	cup apple cider vinegar

Mix meats, bread crumbs and milk together and form into small balls. Place ham balls in casserole.

Mix sauce ingredients together. Cover ham balls with sauce.

Bake at 450° for 1 hour or until browned through. Serve in chafing dish.

Parmesan Puffs

Yields 16

¼	cup milk
¼	cup water
¼	cup butter
¼	teaspoon salt
½	cup all–purpose flour
2	large eggs
1	cup Parmesan cheese, freshly grated
	pepper

Preheat to 400°.

Combine milk, water, butter and salt in small heavy saucepan. Bring mixture to a boil over high heat. Reduce heat to moderate, add flour all at once and beat mixture with a wooden spoon until it leaves the side of the pan and forms a ball.

Transfer mixture to a bowl and whisk in eggs one at a time, whisking well after each addition. Stir in cheese and pepper to taste.

Drop batter in 16 mounds on buttered baking sheet and bake puffs for 20 minutes or until golden brown.

Dough can be made ahead and kept in refrigerator until ready to cook. Puffs are best when baked and served immediately.

Texas Bacon

Serves 25

3	eggs
3	teaspoons vinegar
¾	teaspoon cayenne
1½	teaspoons dry mustard
1	two–pound package extra thick bacon
2	cups bread crumbs

Preheat oven to 350°.

Beat together eggs and add vinegar, cayenne and mustard. Cut bacon strips into thirds. Dip bacon into egg mixture and then into bread crumbs.

Bake on rack in 350° oven for 20 to 30 minutes or until crisp.

Spinach Cheese Canapé

Yields 80 appetizers

4	10–ounce packages frozen chopped spinach
1¼	pounds Feta cheese
1	pound cottage cheese
½	cup Parmesan cheese
¼-½	cup white Cheddar cheese, shredded
4–5	eggs
¾	cup green onion, chopped
	juice of 1 lemon
1	teaspoon dill
¾	teaspoon garlic salt
¾	teaspoon pepper
1½	sticks butter, melted
1	box filo dough

Thaw spinach and use potato ricer or preferred method of removing water from spinach. Mix all ingredients except filo dough in large bowl.

Brush two 9 x 13–inch pans with butter. Place one layer of dough in the first pan and brush again with butter. Repeat until there are 10 layers of dough. Add half of spinach cheese mixture. Again, layer dough and brush with butter 10 times. Repeat process for second pan.

Bake at 350° for one hour. Remove from oven and cut diagonally to create diamond-shaped canapés.

Belgian Endive Hors d'Oeuvre

2	heads Belgian endive
3	yams, baked
2	tablespoons butter, melted
2	tablespoons whipping cream (orange juice may be substituted)
¼	teaspoon nutmeg
6	slices honey cured ham
2	tablespoons currants
	cilantro and parsley

Separate and wash endive leaves. Wrap in towel and refrigerate.

Skin yams and purée with butter, whipping cream, and nutmeg.

Slice ham into small triangles.

On end of each endive leaf, place a mound of yam purée. Top with ham triangle, 2 to 3 currants, and a sprig of cilantro.

Arrange on serving tray, perhaps decorated with orange halves, pierced with cloves and decorated with cilantro and parsley.

Tortilla Roll–ups with Salsa

8	ounces cream cheese
½	cup sour cream
5	scallions, chopped
	juice of ½ lime
1	tablespoon chilies, chopped
1	tablespoon picante sauce, medium hot
6	8–inch flour tortillas
8	ounces picante sauce

Combine cream cheese, sour cream, scallions, lime juice, chilies and 1 tablespoon picante sauce until smooth.

Spread mixture on tortillas and roll up. Cut into ¾–inch pieces. Pass with a dish of picante sauce for dipping.

Roy's Picco de Gallo

½	yellow onion
3	Serrano peppers
10-12	Roma tomatoes
¾	bunch cilantro, chopped
	juice of ½ lime
2	teaspoons sugar or to taste
1	garlic clove, minced
	salt and pepper to taste

Chop onion and peppers in food processor. Leave seeds in for a spicy taste. Add tomatoes. Process until tomatoes are cut, but not mushy. Stir in remaining ingredients.

Roasted Pepper Dip

6	ounces red peppers, roasted
4	ounces jalapeño peppers, chopped
1	cup sour cream
1	cup mayonnaise
1	tablespoon lemon juice
½	teaspoon garlic powder

Purée peppers in food processor or blender. Mix with other ingredients. Refrigerate for one hour to allow flavors to blend.

Serve with cut up vegetables or chips.

Pear and Brie Purses

Serves 12

2	ripe pears, cored and chopped
½	cup pecans, chopped
½	cup coarsely chopped gingersnaps
1½	teaspoons fresh ginger, grated
1	tablespoon brandy
12	sheets phyllo pastry
½	cup unsalted butter, melted
¾	pound Brie cheese
	chives, optional

Preheat oven to 425°.

Combine pears, pecans, gingersnaps, ginger and brandy.

Brush one phyllo sheet with butter and fold lengthwise in half. Brush with butter. Cut crosswise in half.

Cut Brie into 24 equal pieces. Place one piece Brie and 2 tablespoons pear mixture in center of each square. Bring up opposite corners of pastry and twist together to make a purse. Place on baking sheet. Repeat with remaining ingredients.

Bake 10 minutes or until golden. Tie with chive around top of each purse, if desired.

Bengal Cream Cheese

Serves 8

1	8–ounce package cream cheese, softened
3	tablespoons mayonnaise
½	tablespoon curry powder
1	small jar Sun Brand mango chutney, chopped
6	ounces smoked bacon, cooked crisp and chopped
6-8	scallions, finely chopped
	crackers or toast rounds

Whip cream cheese until smooth. Add mayonnaise and curry powder.

Put in ½ inch deep serving dish. Spread chutney over the mixture. Top with bacon and scallions.

Serve with your favorite cracker or toast rounds.

Cran-Raspberry Chutney on Brie

Serves 25

Chutney:

1	cup cranberries
½	cup whole, frozen, unsweetened raspberries, thawed
½	cup honey
½	tart apple, peeled, cored and coarsely chopped
1	medium orange, peeled, pith removed, sliced and seeded
1	small celery stalk, sliced
1	tablespoon water
¼	cup raspberry vinegar
1	teaspoon fresh ginger, grated
2	tablespoons sweet and hot mustard
⅛	teaspoon ground cloves
1	2–pound ripe Brie cheese, well chilled
½	cup toasted almonds, sliced
	Italian parsley for garnish
	crackers or French bread rounds

Combine all chutney ingredients in heavy saucepan. Bring to a boil, stirring frequently. Reduce heat and simmer until mixture thickens and liquid is syrupy, stirring occasionally. Store in refrigerator. Keeps up to 3 weeks.

Cut rind off top of cheese and discard. Cut cheese in half horizontally. Place lower half on baking sheet, cut side up. Spread almonds evenly and top with other half of cheese. Bring to room temperature.

Cover with chutney and bake for 10 minutes or until cheese is soft but not runny. Garnish with parsley and serve with crackers or French bread rounds.

Red Pepper Mascarpone

Yields 30

For a really unusual treat, serve on top of hot pasta!

1	8–ounce jar roasted red peppers, drained
1	garlic clove
8	ounces unsalted butter, softened
8	ounces cream cheese, softened
	crackers

Process peppers and garlic in food processor or blender until smooth. Add butter and cream cheese, a little bit at a time, to food processor or blender until well mixed. Allow to stand in refrigerator for about one hour.

Serve with crackers.

Czechoslovakian Liptauer

Yields 2 cups

Enjoy the compliments!

2	8-ounce packages light cream cheese
2	tablespoons butter, softened
2	tablespoons beer
2	tablespoons capers, chopped
	dash of Dijon mustard
	salt to taste
	paprika for color

Toppings:

daikon and red radishes, chopped
cucumbers, sliced
bacon, fried crisp and crumbled
green onion, chopped
tomatoes, peeled, chopped and seeded
anchovies
sardines

Mix together first 7 ingredients and place in center of large tray.

Surround cheese mixture with radishes, cucumbers, bacon, green onion, tomatoes, anchovies and sardines.

Guests spread cheese on rye rounds and sprinkle on desired toppings.

Zippy Beef and Olive Spread

1	teaspoon instant minced onion
1	tablespoon dry sherry
8	ounces cream cheese
2	tablespoons mayonnaise
3	ounces smoked sliced beef, finely chopped
¼	cup stuffed green olives, chopped

Soften onions in sherry. Blend cream cheese with mayonnaise and add to onions. Stir in beef and olives.

Serve on crackers or rye bread or serve with raw vegetables.

Meat Buns Char Sieu Bow

Yields 32 buns

1	pound lean pork, cut into 1 inch thick steaks

Marinade:

1	large garlic clove, minced
2	tablespoons soy sauce
1	tablespoon sherry
2	tablespoons sugar
1	tablespoon hoisin sauce
1	teaspoon salt

Vegetables:

2	green onions, chopped
1	cup bamboo shoots, cut lengthwise and finely chopped
½	cup Oriental mushrooms, soaked, drained and cut into thin slices, reserving juice
1	cup water chestnuts or jicama, thinly sliced

Sauce:

1	tablespoon sherry
1	teaspoon sugar
2	teaspoons cornstarch
2	tablespoons mushroom water
2	loaves frozen bread dough, thawed
	sesame seeds, optional

Combine garlic, soy sauce, 1 tablespoon sherry, sugar, hoisin sauce and salt. Marinate pork for 2 to 3 hours. Bake on rack at 400° for 30 to 40 minutes. Cool, cut into thin slices and dice.

Sauté onions, bamboo shoots, mushrooms and water chestnuts in wok. Stir–fry briefly.

Make sauce of 1 tablespoon sherry, sugar, cornstarch and water. Add diced meat and set aside to cool.

Cut loaves in half and each half into 8 pieces. Flour hands and shape dough into balls. Stretch balls into rounds. Put 1 rounded tablespoon of filling in center of each round. Pinch edges together around the filling. Place buns seam side down on 2–inch squares of waxed paper. Let rise in a warm spot according to direction on dough package.

Remove from waxed paper and place on baking sheet. Press sesame seeds on top before baking, if desired.

Bake at 375° until golden brown.

Oriental Vegetable Basket

Serves 6

Pretty, delicate appearance.

1	small cucumber
1	small turnip
1	small carrot
	salt to taste
1	cup water
½	cup sugar
⅔	cup rice or distilled vinegar
	rice noodles
	sesame oil

Seed cucumber and dice. Peel and cut turnip and carrot into julienned strips, matchstick size. Sprinkle salt over vegetables that have been tossed together in a bowl. Set aside for 30 minutes. Rinse and drain vegetables.

Combine water, sugar and vinegar in another bowl. Pour over vegetables and gently toss. Chill several hours or overnight.

Drain and serve in individual bamboo steaming baskets lined with chilled rice noodles marinated in sesame oil.

Jicama and Carrot Crudités

Refreshing and low calorie.

1	medium jicama
4 or 5	medium carrots
⅓	cup fresh lime juice
	dash Tabasco
	parsley

Peel and julienne jicama and carrots into 3–inch long, thick pieces. Marinate in lime juice to which Tabasco is added.

Arrange on flat basket alternating carrots and Jicama in circle. Place parsley in center or place a favorite dip in a hollowed-out jicama half encircled by parsley.

> ℮ *Jicama is often referred to as the Mexican potato. This large, bulbous root vegetable has a sweet, nutty flavor and is good both raw and cooked. It contains vitamin C and potassium.*

Steamed Vegetable Platter

Celery Root

Peel outer skin of the root. Cut root in small slivers, slices, or chunks. Toss with enough lemon juice to coat well. Steam until just tender. Toss with lots of fresh pepper, lemon juice, tarragon , mayonnaise, or leave as is.

Broccoli

Break flower parts of broccoli off stem, leaving about ¼–inch stem. Place in steamer, cover and steam until just tender. Peel remaining stem and slice very thin. Steam and toss with the broccoli flowers. Toss with lemon juice or marinate with your favorite dressing.

Cauliflower

Follow directions for above vegetable.

Carrots

Peel carrots and cut off both ends. Using peeler, peel long strips of carrots using as much of the carrot as possible. You should have long, beautiful swirls. Steam for about 2 minutes and toss with crushed ginger and melted butter, margarine or oil.

Zucchini

Scrub well. Cut in quarters lengthwise and slice diagonally. Steam slightly and toss with lemon zest, yogurt and a dash of curry.

Serve platter with a bowl of grated cheese and a bowl of your favorite hollandaise. Especially good if you add a touch of sherry and a dash of dill.

Breads

Open thine eyes and thou shalt be satisfied with bread.

—Proverbs 20:13

Grapenut Bread

Yields 2 loaves

The options are unlimited with the many variations. It's wonderful toasted and freezes beautifully!

2	eggs
2½	cups milk, soured with lemon juice, if desired
1	cup Grapenuts cereal
½	teaspoon salt
1	teaspoon baking soda
2	teaspoons baking powder
1½	cups sugar
3½	cups flour

Variations:

1	cup dried apricots, sliced
1	cup walnuts, chopped
	or
1	cup apple, skin on and chopped
1	cup almonds or walnuts, chopped
1	cup dried pineapple, chopped
1	cup Brazil nuts, chopped
	or
½	cup fresh cranberries, chopped
½	cup fresh pear, chopped
1	cup walnuts, chopped
	or
1	cup wild rice, cooked
1	cup water chestnuts, sliced, or bamboo shoots

Preheat oven to 325° for glass loaf pan, 350° if metal pans are used.

Blend eggs, milk, Grapenuts, salt, baking soda and baking powder in a blender on high speed.

Mix sugar and flour in mixing bowl. Add your choice of variations to dry mixture and stir. Add blender contents to flour mixture. Stir, but do not overbeat. Let sit for 5 minutes.

Put mixture in greased loaf pans. Bake 1 hour or longer if using fresh fruit. Test with wooden skewer. Cool in pans on baking rack for 10 to 15 minutes. Remove from pans. Cool by laying loaves on the side. Cool completely before putting in plastic bags for storage or freezing.

Quick breads are leavened with baking powder or baking soda or both instead of yeast. They do not require kneading or hours to rise. They are the simplest baked goods to prepare and they freeze well.

Sweet and Simple Loaf

Yields 1 loaf

Quick, easy, low-fat and tastes great!

1-2	eggs, or ½ cup egg substitute
1	cup skim milk
1	scant tablespoon canola oil
½	cup real maple syrup
3	cups whole wheat flour
2	teaspoons baking powder
1	teaspoon salt
½	cup raisins

Preheat oven to 350°.

Beat liquid ingredients together. Mix dry ingredients together. Stir dry ingredients into liquid mixture. Fold in raisins.

Pour into loaf pan sprayed with non-stick vegetable spray. Bake for 1 hour or until cake tester comes out clean.

Grandma Tess' Banana Nut Bread

Yields 1 loaf

It stays deliciously moist!

⅓	cup shortening, butter or vegetable preferred
1	cup sugar
2	eggs, well beaten
3	tablespoons sour cream
3	bananas, mashed
1	teaspoon vanilla, if desired
2	cups flour
1	teaspoon soda
1	teaspoon salt
1	cup pecans or walnuts, chopped

Preheat oven to 325°.

Cream shortening, add sugar and beat well. Add eggs, sour cream, bananas and vanilla. Mix well.

Sift flour, soda and salt together. Add to banana mixture and mix well. Stir in nut meats.

Pour into loaf pan and bake for 1 hour or until done.

Buttermilk Loaves

1	cup hot water
1	cup cold buttermilk
1	package dry yeast
1	egg
⅓	cup vegetable oil
⅓	cup sugar
1	teaspoon salt
5½	cups white flour

Combine water and buttermilk in large bowl. Stir. Liquid will be warm. Sprinkle yeast on top.

Mix egg, oil, sugar and salt in small bowl. Add egg mixture to yeast mixture when yeast is dissolved.

Using wooden spoon, beat in 5 cups of flour, 1 cup at a time. Reserve ½ cup flour for kneading.

Knead dough for 5 minutes. Grease dough and place in greased bowl. Cover and let rise for 2 hours. Punch down, flour hands and divide into 4 pieces. Put into four greased, foil pie pans. Let rise for 2 hours or less.

Bake at 375° for 20 minutes in middle of oven, rotating after 10 minutes to brown evenly. Cool on rack for 5 minutes before removing from pans.

Cheese Popovers

3	eggs
1¼	cups milk
1¼	cups sifted flour
¼	teaspoon salt
3	tablespoons butter, melted
I	cup Cheddar cheese, shredded

Preheat oven to 400°.

Beat eggs well with an electric mixer in a large bowl. Beat in milk at low speed. Add flour and salt. Beat until smooth. Stir in melted butter.

Butter popover pan or six custard cups. Fill half full of batter and top with cheese evenly divided among cups. Pour in remaining batter.

Bake for 50 minutes or until puffed and deep golden brown. Let cool in pans for a minute before loosening with knife. Remove and serve hot.

If you prefer popovers with a bit less moisture inside, pierce tops with a fork to release steam before removing from oven.

Herb Onion Batter Bread

Yields 1 loaf

3¼	cups flour
2	packages yeast
2	tablespoons sugar
1	teaspoon salt
½	teaspoon ground sage
¼	teaspoon ground thyme
½	teaspoon rosemary leaves, crushed
2	tablespoons butter or margarine
½	cup onion, finely chopped
⅓	cup warm water
1	egg

Preheat oven to 375°.

Combine 1½ cups of flour, yeast, sugar, salt, sage, thyme and rosemary. Sauté onion in butter until golden. Add to flour mixture.

Add water and egg. Blend with mixer at low speed until moistened. Beat at medium speed for 3 minutes. Stir in remaining flour to make a stiff dough.

Spoon into a greased 2–quart casserole. Cover and let rise in a warm place until doubled in size, about 1 hour. Bake for 35 to 40 minutes until golden brown. Cover the bread with foil if it begins to get too brown.

German Onion Cake

Serves 8 to 10

Wonderful for summer picnics.

1	4–ounce package hot roll mix or your own favorite yeast dough
4	large onions, sliced thin
6	tablespoons butter
2	cups sour cream
3	eggs
½	teaspoon salt
1	tablespoon poppy seeds or ½ cup parsley, chopped

Preheat oven to 350°.

Prepare your own yeast dough or follow directions for hot roll mix. Saute onion slices in butter until transparent. Cool. Beat sour cream with eggs and salt and combine with onions.

Knead dough 10 times when it has doubled in size. Let it rest for 10 minutes. Roll dough out on floured board into a rectangle 11 x 15 inches. Put dough in a greased 9 x 13–inch pan, turning up 1 inch on all sides. Pour onion and sour cream mixture over the dough. Sprinkle with poppy seeds or parsley, if desired.

Bake for 1 hour or until golden brown on top. Cut into 3–inch squares to serve. Can be made ahead, but is best used on the day it is made.

Toasted Pecan Muffins

Yields 12 muffins

These muffins freeze very well!

1½	cups unbleached flour
2	teaspoons baking powder
⅛	teaspoon allspice
¼	teaspoon salt
1¾	cups pecan pieces, toasted
½	cup dark brown sugar, packed
½	cup butter, melted
⅓	cup milk
¼	cup maple syrup
1	egg, room temperature
1	teaspoon vanilla

Preheat oven to 400°.

Mix flour, baking powder, allspice and salt in large bowl. Stir in pecans. Make a well in the dry ingredients.

Whisk together in a bowl the sugar, butter, milk, maple syrup, egg and vanilla. Pour the butter mixture into the well in dry ingredients. Stir until blended. The batter will still be lumpy.

Put paper liners in muffin cups. Fill cups ¾ full. Bake 20 minutes or until tester comes out clean. Serve warm.

Cranberry Yogurt Muffins

Yields 12 large muffins

Great any time of year!

1	cup rolled oats
1	cup plain yogurt
½	cup vegetable oil
¾	cup brown sugar
1	egg
1	cup flour
1	teaspoon salt
½	teaspoon baking soda
1	teaspoon baking powder
1	cup cranberries

Preheat oven to 400°.

Soak oats in yogurt for 5 minutes. Add oil, sugar and egg. Beat well.

Sift in flour, salt, soda and baking powder. Sprinkle cranberries over the flour mixture before stirring to blend.

Fill muffin cups and bake for 20 minutes.

Coconut Carrot Muffins

Yields 6 muffins

Delectable companion for a luncheon salad!

½	cup vegetable oil
⅔	cup pecans
1¾	cups all–purpose flour
½–⅔	cup granulated sugar
½-⅔	cup flaked coconut
2	eggs, slightly beaten
½	cup milk
1	tablespoon baking powder
1	teaspoon cinnamon
⅛	teaspoon cloves
¼	teaspoon salt
1	large carrot, cleaned and grated
½	cup raisins or currants

Preheat oven to 425°.

Combine oil and pecans in a frying pan. Sauté until golden, about 6 minutes. Set aside and cool.

Combine all ingredients including pecans in a food processor. Process for several bursts. Stir once and process for another burst or two. Ingredients will be slightly combined.

Spoon batter into lightly greased muffin cups. Bake for 20 minutes or until muffins are cooked through.

Blueberry Sour Cream Muffins

Yields 12 muffins

Can keep batter in refrigerator many hours before baking.

1	egg, well beaten
1	cup sour cream
1	cup sugar
1¾	cups sifted flour
1	scant teaspoon baking soda
½	teaspoon salt
2	cups blueberries, sprinkled with 1½ tablespoons flour

Preheat oven to 400°.

Combine egg, sour cream and sugar.

Add soda and salt to flour. Combine egg mixture with flour mixture. Fold in blueberries.

Fill greased muffin cups or paper liners ¾ full.

Bake for 20 minutes or until brown.

Andrew's Favorite Bread

Yields 2 large loaves

Good with honey or butter and jam!

2⅔	cups warm water
1	tablespoon yeast
¼	teaspoon sugar
1	tablespoon salt
3	tablespoons gluten flour
½	cup vegetable oil
3	tablespoons molasses
3	cups whole wheat flour
4½	cups unbleached white flour

Sprinkle yeast onto warm water in large bread bowl. Wait several minutes, then sprinkle sugar over water and yeast.

Add salt, gluten flour, vegetable oil and molasses when all the yeast has risen to the surface of the water. Stir in whole wheat flour. Beat with a wooden spoon until smooth.

Add 3 ½ cups of the white flour. Knead dough. Continue to knead dough, adding ¼ cup of flour at a time, until there is no more dry flour. Dough will be firm and bounce back when poked.

Cover dough with a towel. Let dough rise in a warm spot for about 1 hour. Punch down dough and divide into two loaves. Place dough into greased loaf pans. Cover and let rise for 20 minutes or until dough doubles in size.

Put loaves in a cool oven. Bake for 20 minutes at 350°. Bake an additional 20 minutes at 300°. Remove from the oven and cool for at least one hour before putting in plastic bags.

The bread will stay soft and moist if it is not refrigerated.

Josefinas

Yields 30 slices or 16 halves

8	hard rolls
	or
1	thin loaf French bread
1	cup canned green chilies, seeded and chopped
1	cup butter
1	garlic clove, minced
1	cup mayonnaise, light is an option
8	ounces Monterey Jack cheese, grated

Slice rolls into slices or in halves, depending on your size preference. Toast on one side.

Mix chilies with butter and garlic. Spread mixture on untoasted sides of bread.

Mix mayonnaise and cheese. Spread over chili mixture.

Broil until cheese is brown and puffy. Serve at once.

Spicy Pumpkin Raisin Bread

Yields 2 loaves

Bread:

⅓	cup dry sherry
½	cup raisins
1½	cups white sugar
½	cup cooking oil
2	eggs
1	cup pumpkin
1¾	cups flour
¼	teaspoon baking powder
1	teaspoon soda
1	scant teaspoon salt
½	teaspoon ground cloves
1	teaspoon cinnamon
½	teaspoon nutmeg, freshly grated
½	teaspoon ground allspice
½	cup pecan, chopped

Topping:

1	teaspoon cinnamon
¼	cup white sugar
	cup pecan halves to decorate top of loaf

Simmer raisins in sherry for 2 minutes. Set aside and cool.

In large bowl of mixer, beat eggs slightly. Add sugar, oil and pumpkin and mix together.

Sift dry ingredients. Add to pumpkin mixture, using mixer. Fold in raisins, sherry and pecans. Pour into greased loaf pans.

Mix cinnamon and sugar and sprinkle over loaves. Gently press pecans into top, making a design.

Bake at 350° for 1 hour for 8½ x 4–inch loaf pan. For two smaller pans, bake 45 to 55 minutes or until toothpick comes out clean.

Cool for 10 minutes before removing from pan.

If you want a fancier look for your pumpkin bread, try baking in a ring mold or plum pudding pan.

Bread will be a little different every time you make it. That's why bread baking retains an element of magic and mystery. It's always an adventure.

Chive Bread

1	package dry yeast
¼	cup warm water (105° to 115°)
2⅓	cups all–purpose flour, divided
2	tablespoons chives, coarsely chopped
2	tablespoons sugar
1	teaspoon salt
¼	teaspoon baking soda
1	cup sour cream
1	egg
	melted butter or margarine

Preheat oven to 350°.

Dissolve yeast in water in large mixer bowl. Add 1⅓ cups flour and remaining ingredients except melted butter. Beat on low speed for 30 seconds, scraping bowl constantly. Beat on high speed for 2 minutes, again scraping bowl constantly.

Stir in remaining flour. Spread batter evenly in greased 9–inch pie plate. Brush with melted butter and cover. Let rise 50 minutes. Batter will rise but will not double.

Bake bread 40 to 45 minutes or until golden brown.

Taylor's Holiday Morning Ring

18	frozen dough rolls
1	3⅝–ounce package regular butterscotch pudding mix
¾	cup brown sugar, packed
½	cup sweet butter
2	teaspoons cinnamon
½-¾	cup pecan nutmeats

Butter a large bundt pan well. Scatter frozen dough balls inside. Shake the pudding mix over the dough balls.

Melt butter, brown sugar and cinnamon in a small sauce pan. Add pecans and pour mixture over the dough.

Leave uncovered on the kitchen counter after midnight. It will be ready to bake in 350° oven for 30 to 35 minutes when you're ready for your holiday breakfast.

Invert bundt pan onto a large platter quickly after removing from the oven.

Bertha's Lemon Bread

Yields 1 loaf

A delicious, old–fashioned, sweet bread.

3	tablespoons shortening
3	tablespoons butter
1	cup granulated sugar
2	eggs
½	cup milk
1	tablespoon lemon rind, grated
1½	teaspoons baking powder
½	teaspoon salt
1½	cups flour
½	cup walnuts, finely chopped

Syrup:
⅓	cup sugar
3	tablespoons lemon juice

Cream shortening, butter and sugar together in large bowl. Add eggs, milk and lemon rind. Mix well and set aside.

Mix dry ingredients together and add to egg mixture. Stir in nuts. Pour into 9 x 5–inch loaf pan. Let rise for 20 minutes.

Bake at 350° for 45 minutes to 1 hour. Remove from oven and brush with lemon syrup.

Healthy Whole Wheat Bread

Yields 1 loaf

An easy, hearty bread. Wonderful with soups or salads.

2	cups whole wheat flour
1	cup white flour
2	teaspoons baking soda
½	teaspoon salt
1	cup raisins
2	cups low–fat buttermilk
½	cup molasses

Mix dry ingredients. Stir in milk and molasses. Mix thoroughly.

Pour into bread pan. Let stand 1 hour.

Bake at 325° for 1 hour or until cake tester comes out clean.

☻ *Slash the top of your bread with a very sharp knife before it goes into the oven so that it cracks attractively, rather than at random.*

Salads & Dressings

One cook alone cannot make a salad—four persons are needed: a spendthrift for oil, a miser for vinegar, a counselor for salt and a madman to stir it up.

—Anonymous

Green Bean Salad

Serves 6

Substitute other beans, if you like.

1½	pounds green beans, cut into 2–inch pieces
1	teaspoon salt, optional
½	teaspoon dried savory
¾	cup rich chicken broth
4	tablespoons olive oil
2	tablespoons lemon juice
3	tablespoons onion, finely chopped
2	teaspoons fresh dill
2	teaspoons fresh parsley
¼	teaspoon pepper, freshly ground

Cook beans in water with salt and savory until tender crisp or microwave 5 to 6 minutes. Drain and rinse immediately in cold water.

Combine all remaining ingredients in bowl and beat with whisk until well blended. Pour over beans.

Cover and refrigerate. Stir occasionally. Chill at least 2 hours or overnight. Drain beans. Discard marinade.

Fresh Mushroom Salad

Serves 5 to 6

Try different kinds of mushrooms, such as enoki or shiitake.

1	pound fresh mushrooms
	juice of 1 lemon
	salt and black pepper, freshly ground
3	tablespoons oil
3	tablespoons capers

Remove mushroom stems and discard. Wash mushroom caps and dry thoroughly. Slice caps and sprinkle immediately with lemon juice.

Add salt, pepper, oil and capers. Toss lightly.

☙ *Where fairies hold their dances, a magic circle of mushrooms will grow, showing plain as moonlight that there is magic in mushrooms. This magic is glutamate.*

Broccoli Ring Salad

Good with carrots vinaigrette or chicken salad.

1	tablespoon unflavored gelatin
1	can beef broth or consommé
1	small bunch broccoli or 2 packages frozen chopped broccoli, cooked and cooled
4	tablespoons fresh lemon juice
1	tablespoon Worcestershire sauce
½	teaspoon Tabasco
¾	cup mayonnaise
3-4	eggs, hard–boiled and sliced

Dissolve gelatin in ¼ cup of the broth. Add to remaining broth that has been heated. Cool a bit and add the rest of the ingredients.

Pour into a 6–cup, oiled ring mold. Refrigerate until firm.

Unmold and serve on greens.

May be made 1 or 2 days in advance.

Broccoli Salad

Serves 6 to 8

A broccoli must!

1	8–ounce can water chestnuts, sliced
½	cup green pepper, chopped
8	slices bacon, crisp fried and crumbled
1	10–ounce package frozen chopped broccoli, defrosted and drained
4	celery stalks, chopped
2	large tomatoes, chopped
½	large onion, chopped
⅔	cup light mayonnaise
½	teaspoon lemon juice
½	teaspoon sugar
	salt and pepper to taste

Toss all ingredients together.

Refrigerate for at least 20 minutes.

Italian Fennel Salad

Serves 6 to 8

5	cups mixed greens of spinach, romaine and red leaf lettuce
1	fennel bulb
1	6–ounce jar marinated artichokes, drained
1	6–ounce can large, pitted ripe olives, drained and towel dried
¼	cup balsamic vinegar
2	tablespoons lemon juice
	salt and pepper to taste

Rinse and dry greens and break into bite-sized pieces. Place in large salad bowl.

Wash fennel and trim off leaves, mincing 2 tablespoons. Add to greens.

Trim off tough outer stalks of fennel and discard. Cut bulb in half lengthwise and remove core. Cut crosswise into ⅛ inch slices. Add to greens.

Cut artichokes into bite-sized pieces. Add artichokes and olives to salad.

Combine balsamic vinegar and lemon juice. Sprinkle over greens and toss.

Fennel, Apple and Walnut Salad

Serves 4

Rich and delicious!

1	tablespoon white wine or peach vinegar
¼	teaspoon salt
	pepper to taste
½	teaspoon Dijon mustard
3	tablespoons extra virgin olive oil
1	head Boston or Bibb lettuce, washed and dried
½	cup walnuts, toasted for 15 minutes in 250° oven
1	fennel bulb, washed and chopped
1	Granny Smith apple, peeled and sliced
3	tablespoons Roquefort cheese, optional

Make vinaigrette dressing of the first 5 ingredients.

Combine lettuce, walnuts, fennel, apple and cheese. Dress with vinaigrette just before serving.

Celery Root with Mustard Mayonnaise

Serves 4 to 5

3½	cups celery root, about 1 pound
3	tablespoons olive oil
1	tablespoon vinegar
	pinch of salt
¼	teaspoon dry mustard
½	cup mayonnaise
1	tablespoon Dijon mustard
4	tablespoons capers, drained
3	teaspoons chives, chopped
	pinch of tarragon, basil and chervil
	lettuce
	flat leaf parsley

Peel and cut celery root into julienne strips. Marinate overnight in oil, vinegar, salt and dry mustard. Drain.

Mix mayonnaise, Dijon mustard, capers, chives, tarragon, basil and chervil. Add celery root to mayonnaise.

Serve on a bed of lettuce and garnish with flat leaf parsley.

Belgian Endive Salad

Serves 4

2	tablespoons lemon juice
¼	teaspoon salt
¼	cup olive oil
3	heads Belgian endive
½	cup walnuts or pecans, chopped
6	ounces Roquefort cheese, crumbled

Mix first 3 ingredients and pour into salad bowl.

Cut endive lengthwise, then crosswise. Place in salad bowl.

Roast walnuts or pecans. Sprinkle nuts and cheese over endive. Toss and serve.

Chicken Mousse Mold

Serves 6 to 8

Easily prepared in advance.

1	can cream of mushroom soup
1	can chicken stock
1	8–ounce package cream cheese, softened
2	envelopes gelatin
¼	cup chicken stock
1	cup mayonnaise
¾	cup celery, chopped
¼	cup green pepper, chopped
¼	cup yellow pepper, chopped
¼	cup red pepper, chopped
1	large onion, chopped
1	cup chicken, cooked and chopped
1	teaspoon horseradish
1	teaspoon curry powder
	sliced tomatoes
	sliced avocados
	mayonnaise

Heat soup and stock over low heat, stirring to eliminate lumps. Blend in softened cream cheese.

Soften gelatin in ¼ cup stock. Add to soup mixture and dissolve. Cool.

Add remaining ingredients and pour into a 6 to 8–cup greased mold. Chill until set.

Serve with sliced tomatoes, sliced avocados and mayonnaise.

Chicken Salad with Avocados

Serves 6 to 8

6	large chicken breast halves
½	pound heavily smoked crisp bacon, chopped
1	cup celery, chopped
2	avocados, chopped
1½	cups mayonnaise
4	ounces bleu cheese, crumbled
1	tablespoon fresh tarragon leaves

Poach chicken breasts. Cool. Bone, skin and cut into bite-sized pieces.

Combine remaining ingredients. Chill until ready to serve.

Grilled Chicken Salad

Serves 6

This is a tasty, light salad that can be made ahead.

2	whole chicken breasts, boned and grilled
	bleu cheese dressing
2	cups Boston lettuce
2	cups red oak lettuce
2	cups radiccio
1	cup endive, sliced
½	cup watercress or arugula
½	cup bleu cheese, crumbled
¾	cup walnuts, toasted and chopped
1	small red onion, chopped
1	cup red grapes or pomegranate seeds
	lemon caper dressing

Slice chicken breasts and mix with a small amount of bleu cheese dressing.

Wash, dry and layer lettuces, radiccio, endive and watercress on six plates. Divide chicken into 6 portions and place on lettuce. Divide bleu cheese, walnuts, onion and grapes evenly among the 6 servings, sprinkling them on top of chicken.

Dress with additional bleu cheese dressing or lemon caper dressing.

Curried Chicken Salad

Serves 12

Refreshing and light!

6-8	cups chicken, cooked and cubed
1	can water chestnuts, sliced
2	pounds seedless grapes, halved
2-3	cups celery, sliced
2½	cups sliced or slivered almonds, toasted
3	cups mayonnaise
1	tablespoon curry powder
2	tablespoons soy sauce
2	tablespoons lemon juice
	lettuce

Combine chicken, water chestnuts, grapes, celery and 1½ cups of almonds. Reserve 1 cup almonds for garnish. Mix remaining ingredients and add to chicken. Toss well.

Chill several hours and serve on a bed of lettuce. Top with remaining almonds.

Romaine Salad with Swordfish or Tuna

Serves 4

A winner!

¼	cup canola oil
3	tablespoons white tarragon vinegar
1½	teaspoons sugar
⅛	teaspoon tarragon leaves, dried
⅛	teaspoon salt
1	large head romaine lettuce, torn into bite-sized pieces
½	pound small red potatoes, unpeeled
½	pound green beans, trimmed and cut into 2–inch pieces
1	11–ounce can mandarin orange segments, drained
1	2¼–ounce bag slivered almonds, toasted
1	pound swordfish or yellowfin tuna
	salt and pepper to taste

Combine oil, vinegar, sugar, tarragon and salt in jar. Rest mixture 1 hour. Shake well. Coat greens with some of the dressing just before assembling.

Place potatoes in covered, 1–quart round glass casserole. Microwave on high power approximately 4 to 5 minutes or until tender. Cool. Cut each potato into quarters.

Steam green beans until tender crisp. Drain and cool.

Put romaine, potatoes, green beans, almonds and oranges into large salad bowl. Toss with dressing. Divide among four plates.

Broil or grill fish and season to taste. Cut fish while still hot into 1½ inch pieces and serve on top of prepared salads.

Cold Sliced Tomatoes with Mozzarella Cheese

tomatoes, cold and sliced
mozzarella cheese, sliced
fresh basil, chopped
extra-virgin olive oil

Alternate tomatoes and cheese on a platter.

Drizzle with oil and sprinkle basil over top.

Cutting tomatoes in vertical slices preserves more of the juice.

Shrimp and Bean Salad

Serves 4 to 5

A tasty combination!

1¼	pounds fresh green beans
1	red onion, chopped
¾	pound bacon
½	lemon
1	pound raw shrimp
2	medium tomatoes, peeled, seeded and diced
3	tablespoons olive oil
1	tablespoon red wine vinegar
	salt and freshly ground pepper

Boil beans until tender-crisp.

Drain and rinse in ice water. Drain again and dry. Put onions and beans in large bowl. Cover and chill for 2 hours.

Fry bacon until crisp. Drain on paper towel. Crumble and set aside.

Place lemon and shrimp in boiling water. Return water to boil. Remove shrimp and cool. Peel and cut shrimp into ½ –¾ inch dice.

Add bacon, shrimp, tomatoes and olive oil to onion and bean mixture. Add vinegar. Season to taste with salt and pepper. Mix very thoroughly.

Shrimp in Papaya Boats

Serves 4

2	ripe papayas, peeled and cut in halves
2	cups shrimp, cooked and cut lengthwise
½	cup mayonnaise
1	teaspoon fresh lemon juice
1	teaspoon hot curry powder
1	tablespoon apple juice
	few dashes onion juice
	Bibb lettuce
	watercress

Peel papayas carefully. Cut in half and remove seeds. Set aside.

Mix mayonnaise with lemon juice, curry powder, onion juice and apple juice. Toss shrimp in mayonnaise mixture and fill papayas.

Serve on a bed of lettuce and watercress.

Excellent summer salad served with toasted English muffins topped with a slice of tomato and grated Cheddar cheese. Broil muffins until the cheese melts.

Spinach Salad with Chicken

Serves 6 to 8

3	bunches spinach, washed and torn
½	cup raisins
½	cup pecans, toasted
3	firm apples, cubed
2	tablespoons sesame seeds, toasted
½	cup green onions, chopped
½	cup celery, chopped
1-2	whole chicken breasts, cooked and shredded

Dressing:

⅓	cup vinegar
⅔	cup oil
¼	cup water
2	tablespoons chutney, chopped
1	teaspoon dry mustard
1	teaspoon curry powder
1	teaspoon Tabasco
1	teaspoon seasoned salt

Mix spinach, raisins, pecans, apples, sesame seeds, onions, celery and chicken in bowl.

Mix vinegar, oil, water, chutney, mustard, curry powder, Tabasco and seasoned salt in small bowl. Stir well.

Combine ingredients of the two bowls and toss gently.

Greens with Basil Vinaigrette

Serves 6 to 8

2-3	cups chicory
2-3	cups Boston lettuce
2	tablespoons white wine vinegar
2	tablespoons shallots, finely chopped
2	tablespoons parsley, finely chopped
	pinch of dried thyme, crumbled
1	teaspoon dried basil or 1 tablespoon fresh basil, chopped
4	tablespoons olive oil
	salt and pepper to taste

Whisk oil and vinegar in large bowl. Add shallots and herbs. Toss with greens.

Serve with Goat Cheese Croutons* on the side.

Flaming Spinach and Bacon Salad

Serves 6 to 8

Very dramatic!

1	pound spinach or any soft leaf green
½	bunch watercress
1	small sweet red onion, peeled and thinly sliced in rings
6	bacon slices, diced
¼	cup vinegar
1	teaspoon sugar
3	tablespoons brandy

Garnish:

slivered almonds or pine nuts
hard-cooked egg, thinly sliced
green pepper rings, thinly sliced
slivers of ham or tuna
shredded cheese
apple or pear slices

Wash spinach and watercress or other greens thoroughly. Pinch off stems. Drain and dry greens thoroughly. Combine greens in large bowl with red onion.

Cook diced bacon in blazer pan of chafing dish until crisp. Add vinegar and sugar and bring to a boil while stirring.

Add greens and toss over low heat until wilted. Lift greens from dressing to hot platter with fork and spoon.

Add brandy to drippings in blazer pan. Heat, ignite and pour over salad.

Garnish salad after flaming with any or all of the last six ingredients.

Classic Vinaigrette

1	tablespoon Dijon mustard
1	garlic clove, finely minced
	salt and pepper to taste
3	tablespoons white wine vinegar
3	tablespoons olive oil
3	tablespoons vegetable oil

Add garlic to mustard. Season with salt and pepper. Add vinegar. Stir to dissolve.

Whisk oil in steady stream to emulsify.

The Marsh Dressing

1	cup red wine vinegar
2	tablespoons Dijon mustard
2	green onions
1	cup fresh parsley, loosely packed
1	teaspoon pepper, freshly ground
1	tablespoon honey
½	teaspoon salt
1	teaspoon basil
½	teaspoon garlic
2	cups canola oil

Combine ingredients, except oil, in blender. Blend until smooth.

With motor running, slowly add oil.

This dressing may be thinned with up to ½ cup water.

Christmas Salad

Serves 6

2	cans hearts of palm
1	red pepper, finely diced
1	green pepper, finely diced
6	whole leaves romaine lettuce
2	pomegranates

Cut hearts of palm into ¼-inch pieces. Mix with red and green peppers. Divide into 6 equal portions. Place mixture on romaine leaf on salad plate.

Peel pomegranates. Decorate each plate with pomegranate seeds.

Drizzle Raspberry Vinaigrette* on top of each salad.

Raspberry Vinaigrette

Serves 6

1	cup corn oil
⅓	cup raspberry vinegar
1	teaspoon Dijon mustard
2	teaspoons black pepper, freshly ground
1	teaspoon salt
2	garlic cloves

Mix all ingredients. Allow to stand at room temperature for one hour.

Pale Summer Salad

Serves 8 to 10

A summer favorite.

Dressing:

⅓	cup good olive oil
⅓	cup tarragon vinegar
	juice of ½ lemon
1	teaspoon sea salt
1	tablespoon pepper, freshly ground
1	pinch sugar

Salad:

½	cup green seedless grapes, cut in halves
¾	cup cucumber, peeled and thinly sliced
5	green onions, chopped
½	bok choy, cleaned and chopped
½	head lettuce, cleaned and torn into small pieces
½	cup fine bread crumbs
½	cup Asiago cheese, grated
½	large jicama, sliced into thin pieces 2 inches long

Combine dressing ingredients.

Place grapes, cucumber and onions in dressing. Marinate at least an hour.

Combine bok choy and lettuce with cucumber mixture. Toss well, coating each leaf with dressing. Toss with bread crumbs. Toss again lightly with cheese and sprinkle jicama on top.

Serve icy cold with cold utensils.

Cucumber Salad

Best with English cucumbers.

1½	medium cucumbers, peeled if desired
2	teaspoons salt
1	medium red onion, thinly sliced

Dressing:

¾	cup cider or white vinegar
2	tablespoons sugar dissolved in 2 tablespoons water
1	teaspoon salt
¼	teaspoon pepper, freshly ground
2	tablespoons fresh dill, chopped

Slice cucumber paper thin. Sprinkle with salt. Drain in colander ½ hour. Wash off salt and pat dry. Mix cucumber with thinly sliced onion in a bowl.

Mix dressing and toss with cucumber and onion.

Spinach and Fruit with Raspberry Vinaigrette

Serves 6

Destined to be a new classic.

2	10–ounce packages fresh spinach, stems trimmed, washed and patted dry
4	ounces feta cheese, cubed
1	cup dried apricots, sliced
2	ripe pears, cored and sliced
1	cup pecans, toasted

Vinaigrette:

1	package frozen raspberries, thawed and drained
2	tablespoons sherry vinegar
2	tablespoons fresh lemon juice
½	cup olive oil
½	cup crème fraîche
	salt and freshly ground white pepper to taste

Process raspberries in food processor until puréed. Strain through sieve to remove seeds and return purée to processor. Add vinegar and lemon juice

Add oil in a thin stream. Add crème fraîche and process until smooth. Season to taste.

Place cheese, fruits, and nuts on bed of spinach leaves. Drizzle with vinaigrette.

Ginger Pear Mold

Serves 5 or 6

Best when made with strong ginger ale.

1	3-ounce package lemon gelatin
1	cup boiling water
⅔	cup ginger ale
1	tablespoon fresh lemon juice
1	tablespoon orange rind, grated
¼	teaspoon salt
1	cup pears, diced
¼	cup seeded grapes
2	tablespoons candied ginger, chopped
¼	cup broken pecans
	fresh greens

Dissolve gelatin in water. Cool slightly. Add ginger ale and chill until thickened.

Fold in remaining ingredients. Pour into 3½ cup mold or 5 individual ⅔ cup molds.

Serve on a bed of greens.

Holiday Salad

Serves 6

⅔	cup frozen cranberry-raspberry juice concentrate, thawed
⅔	cup dried tart cherries
½	cup raspberry vinegar
½	cup walnut oil
2½	tablespoons crème de cassis
	ground pepper to taste
1	tablespoon crème fraîche or sour cream
4	bunches watercress
½	cup walnut halves, toasted

Plump dried cherries in concentrate in small bowl for one hour.

Whisk together vinegar, oil and cassis in another small bowl. Add pepper and crème fraîche. Whisk again and set aside.

Toss watercress in salad bowl with dressing just before serving. Divide among six salad plates.

Remove cherries from bowl with slotted spoon. Sprinkle cherries and walnuts on each salad.

Cranberry, Apple and Pecan Salad

Serves 6 to 8

Very refreshing!

2	cups cranberries
1	cup orange juice
	rind of 1 orange, grated
½	cup sugar
4	cloves
1	medium apple, cored and coarsely chopped
½	cup pecans, chopped
	lettuce leaves

Combine cranberries with orange juice, rind, sugar and cloves in medium saucepan. Cook over medium heat just until the cranberries pop, about 2 minutes. Remove cloves.

Pour cranberries and juice into bowl. Add apple and pecans. Toss gently to combine. Chill salad before serving on lettuce leaves.

 With an apple, I will astonish Paris.

—Paul Cézanne

Pear Salad

Serves 6

⅓	cup canola oil
2	tablespoons wine vinegar
1	teaspoon lemon juice
½	teaspoon lemon zest
1	teaspoon Dijon mustard
½	teaspoon salt
	pepper to taste
4	cups assorted greens
3	pears, sliced
⅓	cup hazelnuts, chopped and toasted

Mix oil, vinegar, lemon juice, lemon zest, mustard, salt and pepper together. Whisk well.

Combine greens and toss with dressing. Top with pear slices and hazelnuts.

Warm Cabbage and Goat Cheese Salad

Serves 4 to 6

1	small head red cabbage
¼	cup olive oil
1	small onion, minced
	juice of 1 lemon
4	tablespoons balsamic vinegar
3	tablespoons capers
3	ounces goat cheese, diced
⅓	cup pine nuts, roasted
3	tablespoons parsley, minced

Cut cabbage leaves into julienne strips. Sauté cabbage and onion in olive oil until wilted, but still crunchy. Add lemon juice, vinegar and capers. Toss. Remove from heat. Season with salt and pepper.

Transfer to serving bowl. Sprinkle with goat cheese, pine nuts and parsley. Serve warm.

> *Goat cheese or chèvre is made from pure white goat's milk and has a delightfully tart flavor. Imported cheese with "Pur chèvre" on the label ensures that the cheese is made entirely from goat's milk.*

Red Cabbage and Avocado Salad

4	cups red cabbage, finely chopped
1	medium avocado, chopped
	lemon juice
4	tablespoons onion, finely chopped
¼	pound bleu or Roquefort cheese
¼	teaspoon salt
	dash of Tabasco sauce
1	teaspoon Worcestershire sauce
2	tablespoons cider vinegar
1	tablespoon tarragon vinegar
½	cup salad oil
1	cup celery, diced
½	teaspoon salt
	dash of pepper
2	hard-boiled eggs, chopped

Marinate avocado in lemon juice for a short time to prevent discoloration.

Make dressing by mashing cheese and blending in salt, Tabasco, Worcestershire and vinegars. Beat thoroughly. Add salad oil slowly and blend well.

Toss cabbage, avocado, onion, celery and eggs. Pour on dressing. Season with salt and pepper. Chill for at least ½ hour.

Cabbage Salad

2-4	cups cabbage, chopped
¼	cup green onions, chopped
1	package chicken ramen noodle mix
½	cup salted sunflower nuts
¼	cup almonds, chopped

Dressing:

¼	cup oil
2	tablespoons red wine vinegar
2	tablespoons sugar
	seasoning packet from noodle mix

Mix cabbage and onions together. Break noodles with knife handle in plastic bag.

Mix oil, vinegar, sugar and seasoning packet. Chill.

Add sunflower nuts, almonds and noodles to cabbage mixture when ready to serve.

Add dressing last.

Gazpacho Mold

Serves 8

2	envelopes unflavored gelatin
3	cups tomato juice
¼	cup wine vinegar
1	garlic clove, minced
2	teaspoons salt
	dash cayenne
2	tomatoes, peeled, seeded, chopped and drained
½	cup onion, chopped
¾	cup green pepper, chopped
¾	cup cucumber, seeded and chopped

Soften gelatin in 1 cup tomato juice. Bring to boil. Remove from heat and add remaining ingredients.

Place in oiled ring mold. Refrigerate until set.

Serve with mayonnaise or avocado dip.

Cold Wild Rice Salad

Serves 16

Prepare at least two days prior to serving.

3	cups wild rice
	chicken stock
8	green onions, including stems, thinly sliced
1	jar pimento, drained and finely diced
1½	cups Italian dressing
½	cup salted sunflower nuts

Cook rice in chicken stock about 1 hour until fluffy. Drain. Add onions and pimento. Toss with Italian dressing and refrigerate. Stir occasionally.

Add sunflower nuts just before serving.

Add chicken, turkey or seafood for a main course salad.

❸ *Wild rice, known for its luxurious nutty flavor, isn't really rice at all. In actuality, it is long–grain marsh grass native to the northern Great Lakes area, where it is harvested by local Native American Indians.*

Wild Rice, Walnut and Fresh Cranberry Salad

erves 4 to 6

dd shredded, cooked chicken,
urkey, duck or Virginia ham
r a main course salad.

½	cup cranberries
½	cup water
2	cups wild rice, cooked
½	cup celery, chopped
¼	cup green onions, chopped
½	cup pecans, chopped and toasted
	lettuce

Dressing:

⅓	cup walnut oil
¼	cup raspberry vinegar
1	teaspoon sugar
1	teaspoon Dijon mustard
	salt and freshly ground pepper to taste

Cook cranberries in water over medium heat until they pop, about 2 minutes. Drain.

Combine next 4 ingredients with cranberries in large bowl.

Whisk together oil, vinegar, sugar, mustard, salt and pepper in small bowl. Pour over salad and toss gently.

Serve on lettuce leaves at room temperature.

Tabbouleh

Serves 4 to 6

A great summer side dish
with chicken or lamb.

1	cup bulgar
2	cups boiling water
2	cubes chicken bouillon
2	tomatoes, finely diced
1	bunch green onions, finely chopped
1	cup fresh mint, chopped
2	cups parsley, finely chopped
½	cup fresh lemon juice
½	cup olive oil
2	teaspoons salt
	pepper to taste

Place bulgar in bowl with bouillon cubes. Pour boiling water over the bulgar mixture and let stand at least 1 hour. Drain.

Add remaining ingredients and chill.

Couscous–Quinoa Salad with Lemon Dressing

Serves 4 to 6

This salad is ideal for advance preparation.

½	cup quinoa
1	cup water
½	cup couscous
½	cup water or vegetable stock, hot
1	stalk celery, diced
1	scallion, chopped
2	tablespoons fresh parsley, chopped
⅓	cup currants

Dressing:

¼	cup fresh lemon juice
1	tablespoon olive oil
1	tablespoon water
¼	teaspoon cinnamon
¼	teaspoon black pepper
¼	teaspoon turmeric
	few drops of hot pepper sauce

Rinse quinoa thoroughly in fine strainer and drain. Place quinoa and 1 cup water in medium saucepan. Bring water to a boil. Reduce heat to medium, cover, and simmer until water is absorbed, about 8 minutes. Grains will be translucent and outer ring will separate when done.

Stir together couscous and hot water or vegetable stock in medium bowl. Cover and let stand until liquid is completely absorbed, 5 to 10 minutes.

Combine lemon juice, oil, water, cinnamon, pepper, turmeric and pepper sauce in small bowl.

Prepare remaining salad ingredients.

Fluff couscous with fork after it has softened. Stir in quinoa and combine with salad ingredients. Add dressing. Toss again.

Serve immediately or allow to cool. If prepared in advance, remove from refrigerator about 30 minutes before serving.

To add variety: use all couscous or all quinoa; substitute cooked brown rice for the couscous and quinoa; add other vegetables such as tomato cubes or steamed, cut asparagus; or add cooked chicken cubes or baby shrimp.

Cranberry Ramekins

Serves 8

2	packages strawberry gelatin
2	cups water, boiling
8	ounces cream cheese, cubed
1	cup cranberry sauce

Dissolve 1 package gelatin in one cup of boiling water. Stir well and place in blender with cream cheese. Blend until smooth. Pour into 8 well–oiled ramekins or use non–stick spray. Chill until set.

Dissolve second package of gelatin in remaining cup of boiling water. Add cranberry sauce. Leave on heat until well blended. Pour over top of ramekins. Chill until firm, about 4 hours.

Unmold and garnish with Candied Cranberries*.

Candied Cranberries

2	cups water
2	cups sugar
8	ounces fresh cranberries

Mix sugar and water in large pan. Bring to boil. Add cranberries and reduce heat. Simmer for 10 minutes. Cool.

Drain off syrup. Spread cranberries on cookie sheet. Allow to stand for 2 to 3 hours. Use as garnish.

Dust berries with granulated sugar for effect, if desired.

🍃 *These shiny scarlet berries are grown in huge, sandy bogs on low trailing vines. They are also called bounceberries, because ripe ones bounce.*

Soups

Soup is to dinner what a portico is to a palace or an overture to an opera.

—Grimod de la Reynière

Cold Cranberry Soup

Serves 6 to 8

A tart and refreshing first or final course.

1	pound cranberries, fresh or frozen
	juice of 4 oranges
1	tablespoon orange zest, chopped
	juice of 2 lemons
1½	teaspoons lemon zest, chopped
⅓	cup brandy
3	whole cloves
1	cinnamon stick
¼	teaspoon nutmeg, freshly grated
2	cups half and half
1	cup sour cream or crème fraîche

Simmer cranberries in fresh juices, zests, brandy and spices. There should be enough juice to cover berries. Simmer 20 minutes or until thick.

Purée and strain using a very fine sieve. Adjust seasonings. Add nutmeg. Cool and add cream. Refrigerate.

May be prepared one or two days before serving.

Swirl a dollop of crème fraîche into a pattern on bright crimson soup when ready to serve.

ϴ *When cooking with cloves or other spices, put them in a small cheesecloth bag for easy retrieval.*

Strawberry Soup

Serves 4

½	cup sugar
1	tablespoon cornstarch
2	pints fresh strawberries, hulled
1	cup orange juice
1	cup dry red wine
1	8–ounce carton sour cream

Stir sugar and cornstarch together in saucepan. Blend strawberries and orange juice in food processor. Add to sugar mixture.

Add wine and cook over medium heat until thickened. Stirring continuously, cook for 2 more minutes. Remove from heat and stir in sour cream. Transfer to covered container. Refrigerate for 10 to 24 hours.

Serve in bowls garnished with strawberries.

Melon Gazpacho

Yields 8 cups

A delightfully refreshing summer soup with zing!

4	cups cantaloupe or honeydew melon, diced
1	large carrot, shredded
2	cucumbers, peeled and diced
8	green onions, thinly sliced
1/3	cup sherry vinegar
1	cup orange juice
1/2	teaspoon white pepper
2	tablespoons lemon juice
	fresh mint leaves

Process all the melon and half of the carrots, cucumbers and onions in food processor. Reserve remaining vegetables to blend with melon mixture for texture.

Blend together sherry vinegar, orange juice, white pepper, lemon juice and reserved vegetables in a separate bowl. Stir in the melon mixture. Chill thoroughly.

Garnish each serving with a mint leaf.

Shrimp Gazpacho

Serves 4

Can be made a day before serving.

1	quart Clamato juice
1/3	cup unpeeled cucumber, chopped
2	tablespoons scallions, thinly sliced
2	tablespoons olive oil
2	tablespoons red wine vinegar
1	tablespoon sugar
1½	tablespoons fresh dill, chopped
1/2	teaspoon Tabasco
1/4	pound small salad shrimp

Combine all ingredients except shrimp. Add shrimp just before serving.

Serve chilled.

Gazpacho has been described as "the national soft drink of Spain". It is nothing if it is not refrigerated for at least 24 hours, so the vegetable juices can mingle with the aromatics.

Carrot Soup

Serves 8

Serve hot or cold.

1	cup leeks, sliced
1	cup onions, coarsely chopped
2	tablespoons butter
3	cups chicken stock
1	pound carrots, peeled and sliced
1	potato, peeled and sliced
⅛	teaspoon white pepper
1	tablespoon lemon Mrs. Dash seasoning
3–4	teaspoons fresh ginger, chopped
1	garlic clove, minced
1	cup buttermilk
1	cup half and half
1	cup plain yogurt
	chives, croutons or thin slices of carrot

Sauté leeks and onions in butter until slightly translucent. Add stock, vegetables, seasonings and garlic. Simmer covered about 15 minutes until vegetables are tender and soft. Cool.

Purée in blender in batches with the buttermilk, half and half and yogurt.

Serve hot or cold. Garnish with chives, croutons or thin slices of carrot.

Cold Chive Tomato Soup

Serves 6

2	cans tomato soup
3	cups whole or skim milk
1	cup heavy cream or half and half
1	tablespoon basil
2	teaspoons low sodium soy sauce
2	tablespoons lime juice
1	tablespoon celery salt
2	tablespoons chives, chopped

Add milk and cream slowly to tomato soup. Add the basil, soy sauce, lime juice and celery salt. Mix well.

Serve with chive garnish.

Green Pea and Lettuce Soup

Serves 6

1	onion, diced
2	tablespoons oil or butter
1	medium potato, diced
2	cups chicken broth
2	teaspoons curry powder to taste
1	teaspoon fresh lemon juice
	salt and pepper to taste
1	10–ounce package frozen peas
1	head lettuce, chopped
	milk or cream as needed
	chives, chopped

Sauté onion in oil, in large pot, until translucent. Add potato, chicken broth, curry, lemon juice, salt and pepper. Cook for 5 minutes. Add peas and cook for 10 minutes. Add lettuce and warm through until lettuce is completely wilted.

Blend in food processor or blender until smooth. Add milk or cream if too thick. Garnish with chopped chives or a chiffonade of lettuce.

Serve hot or cold.

Tomato Yogurt Soup

Serves 8

1½	cups plain yogurt
3	tablespoons lemon juice
1	tablespoon vinegar
	salt to taste
9	cups tomato juice
1	tablespoon curry powder
2	cucumbers, chopped or sliced
	pepper to taste
	fresh parsley, chopped, for garnish

Beat yogurt in a large bowl until smooth. Add lemon juice, vinegar and salt. Stir to blend thoroughly.

Stir in tomato juice. Add curry powder, cucumber and pepper. Cover and refrigerate for at least 4 hours. Garnish and serve.

Watercress Vichyssoise

Serves 6

1	tablespoon butter
3	tablespoons olive oil
3	leeks, white part only, chopped
2	medium potatoes, peeled and cut in chunks
5	cups chicken stock, fresh or canned
1	teaspoon salt
¼	teaspoon pepper
1	bunch watercress, stems removed
1	cup light cream
	sprigs of watercress

Heat butter and olive oil in a large saucepan over low heat. Add leeks and sauté 20 minutes. Add potatoes, stock, salt and pepper. Simmer 20 minutes. Add watercress and simmer 10 minutes. Cool soup slightly.

Pour in cream. Purée in blender until smooth. Return soup to saucepan and heat thoroughly.

Serve hot. Garnish each bowl with a sprig of watercress.

May also be served cold. Chill in refrigerator before serving.

Cold Watercress Soup

Serves 4

1	tablespoon unsalted butter
½	cup leek, white part only, chopped
¼	cup onion, chopped
1	garlic clove, minced
1½	cups chicken stock
1	cup cooked potato, diced
1½	cups watercress
½	cup skim milk
	salt and pepper to taste
1	tablespoon parsley, chopped

Sauté leek, onion and garlic in butter until wilted, about 5 minutes. Add stock and potato. Bring to boil. Reduce heat. Add watercress and simmer 5 minutes.

Purée soup in blender, adding skim milk. Season with salt and pepper. Chill.

Garnish with chopped parsley.

Supper Soup

Serves 6 generously

2	tablespoons olive oil
1	medium onion, chopped
1½	pounds lean ground beef
1	medium eggplant, diced
1	garlic clove, minced
1	cup celery, chopped
1	28–ounce can peeled tomatoes, coarsely chopped
2	10½–ounce cans beef broth
1	teaspoon salt
1	teaspoon pepper
1	teaspoon sugar
1	tablespoon Worcestershire sauce
1	teaspoon dried basil
¾	cup macaroni
2	tablespoons parsley, minced
	Parmesan cheese, grated
	or
	Asiago cheese, shredded

Sauté onion in oil until golden in heavy pot. Add meat. Stir until it is no longer pink. Drain excess fat.

Add eggplant, garlic, celery, tomatoes, broth, salt, pepper, sugar, Worcestershire and basil. Cover and simmer for 30 minutes. Add macaroni and parsley. Simmer 10 minutes.

Serve in heated bowls and top with cheese.

Apple Broccoli Soup

Serves 4

Excellent served warm in the winter and chilled in summer!

2	tablespoons butter or margarine
1	small yellow onion, thinly sliced
1	large Golden Delicious apple, peeled, cored and chopped
¾	pound broccoli
2	cups chicken stock or canned chicken consommé
	salt and white pepper to taste
	plain yogurt

Cook onion and apple in butter until soft, about 5 minutes, in a medium saucepan.

Peel broccoli and separate flowerets. Chop the stems coarsely. Add stock and broccoli to saucepan. Bring to a boil and simmer, uncovered, until broccoli is tender. Cool slightly. Whirl in blender or food processor until smooth.

Reheat over low heat and season to taste. Garnish each serving with a dollop of yogurt.

Herbed Eggplant Soup

Serves 6

An excellent microwave recipe.

3	tablespoons olive oil
3	garlic cloves, finely chopped
1	large onion, chopped
1	cup celery, chopped
2	medium eggplants, peeled and cubed
1	teaspoon salt
	pepper, freshly ground, to taste
1	16–ounce can whole, peeled tomatoes, chopped
2	tablespoons fresh parsley, chopped
1½	teaspoons fresh basil, minced, or ½ teaspoon dried
1½	teaspoons fresh oregano, minced, or ½ teaspoon dried
¾	teaspoon fresh thyme leaves or ¼ teaspoon dried
3½	cups chicken broth
¾	cup dry sherry, divided
	Parmesan cheese, freshly grated for garnish, if served hot
	sour cream and chopped fresh chives, for garnish, if served cold

Place oil, garlic, onion, celery, eggplant, salt and pepper in a 5–quart microwave casserole. Stir well and cover. Microwave on high for 15 minutes. Stir every 5 minutes.

Add tomatoes and juice, parsley, basil, oregano and thyme. Stir and recover. Microwave for 8 minutes. Stir after 4 minutes. Stir in broth and recover. Microwave on high for 15 to 17 minutes or until vegetables are tender. Stir in ½ cup sherry, recover. Microwave on high for 5 minutes.

Purée half the soup in food processor or blender. Return puréed soup to casserole. Stir in remaining ¼ cup sherry. Reheat if necessary.

If served hot, ladle into bowls and sprinkle with Parmesan cheese. If served cold, place a dollop of sour cream on each filled bowl and sprinkle with chives.

Grow your own eggplant in pots. Pinch off tops of plant when it is ten inches high. When five or six flowers appear, remove the remaining flowers and feed with liquid organic fertilizer every ten days.

Oriental Spinach Soup

4	cups beef broth
2	teaspoons fresh ginger, grated
1	garlic clove, minced
2	green onions, chopped
2	tablespoons soy sauce
	pinch of sugar
½	pound lean ground beef
3	cups fresh spinach, coarsely chopped
½	pound firm tofu, cubed
1	can minced clams and broth
2	tablespoons sesame seeds, toasted

Heat broth. Add ginger, garlic, onions, soy sauce and sugar. Break up ground beef into broth. Cook slowly for 15 minutes.

Add spinach, tofu, clams, broth and sesame seeds. Cook just until spinach is tender.

Serve immediately.

☻ *Wash spinach in salted water and repeated washings will not be necessary.*

Fresh Spinach Soup

1	pound fresh spinach
⅓	cup shallots, chopped
2	tablespoons butter
2	14–ounce cans chicken broth
¼–½	teaspoon nutmeg, freshly grated
	salt and pepper to taste
¼	cup cream
1	egg yolk
1	egg, hard boiled

Wash spinach well. Remove stems. Steam spinach for 3 to 4 minutes until wilted. Refresh spinach in very cold water. Squeeze dry.

Sauté shallots in butter until limp. Purée spinach, shallots and chicken broth in blender. Pour into saucepan. Season with salt, pepper and nutmeg. Simmer until heated through.

Whisk cream and egg yolk together and stir into soup. Mince or sieve boiled egg and use for garnish.

Caraway Cabbage Soup
with Lemon Dill Spaetzle

Serves 6

2	quarts smoked ham stock, clarified

Garnish:

2	cups cabbage, shredded and blanched
1	cup onions, shredded
1	teaspoon caraway seeds
½	cup tomatoes, diced
½	cup carrots, julienned
1	teaspoon dill, chopped

Spaetzle:

1	pound flour
½	ounce salt
4	eggs
1	cup milk
½	cup water
1	teaspoon dill, chopped
	zest of lemon

Heat ham stock thoroughly. Prepare garnish.

Sift flour and salt into bowl. Make well in flour.

Combine lukewarm milk and water with eggs. Pour into well and stir until combined. Add lemon and dill. Beat dough until bubbles start to form.

Force dough through colander into boiling salted water. Remove noodles when they float. Add spaetzle and garnish to soup.

❧ *Caraway, a member of the parsley family, resembles Queen Anne's Lace. Its root is edible, like a delicate parsnip; the leaves have a similar flavor and are milder than the seeds. Caraway seed is refreshing; it has a clean cut pungency, which lightens and cuts heavy kinds of food such as pork, liver, cabbages and cheese.*

Positively Perfect Pumpkin Soup

Particularly festive when served in mini–pumpkins as bowls.

mini–pumpkins
strong chicken broth, 3 bouillon cubes to 1 cup water
half and half
crushed cardamom seeds, to taste
mini–pumpkins for serving

Preheat oven to 350°.

Prepare pumpkins for baking by cleaning, removing stems and cutting in half. Bake for 35 to 40 minutes. Cool slightly and scoop out flesh. Pumpkin flesh may be frozen for up to three days if prepared in advance.

Purée pumpkin with chicken broth using a ratio of 1 cup pumpkin to ¾ cup broth. Let mixture rest overnight in refrigerator.

Heat purée. Add about ½ cup cream per 1 cup mixture. Season with cardamom and serve in cleaned mini–pumpkins.

Crème de Broccoli Supreme

Serves 3 to 4

1	medium onion, chopped
1	package chopped frozen broccoli or fresh equivalent
1	cup chicken broth
1	teaspoon nutmeg
1	can cream of mushroom soup
2	tablespoons sherry or more to taste
1	teaspoon curry powder
1	cup sour cream, optional

Cook onion and broccoli in chicken broth with nutmeg until tender–crisp. Combine with mushroom soup.

Blend in food processor or blender. Add seasonings and sherry. Add sour cream, if desired. Blend briefly.

May be served hot or cold.

Minestrone with Pesto Sauce

Serves 8 to 10

2	cups dried white beans, great Northern or cannellini
	cold water to cover
2	teaspoons salt
½	teaspoon black pepper, freshly ground
¼	cup olive oil
1	cup celery, chopped
1	cup onion, chopped
1	cup carrot, chopped
2	garlic cloves, pressed
1	1–pound 14–ounce can Italian tomatoes
¼	cup parsley, minced
½	teaspoon basil
½	teaspoon thyme
½	teaspoon bay leaf, crushed
2	10½–ounce cans condensed chicken broth

Garnish:

2	cups cabbage, shredded
2–3	zucchini, sliced
1	cup broken macaroni

Soak beans overnight in water to cover. Drain and cover with fresh water. Bring to boil. Reduce heat. Add salt and pepper. Cover and simmer 1 hour. Do not drain.

Sauté celery, onion and carrot in oil. Add garlic.

Add sautéed vegetables, tomatoes, parsley, basil, thyme, bay leaf and chicken broth to beans. Continue cooking until beans are tender, about 1 hour.

For advance preparation, stop at this point and refrigerate. Reheat before continuing.

Add cabbage, zucchini and macaroni to soup. Simmer, uncovered, for 15 minutes, stirring occasionally.

Ladle into soup bowls. Pass *Pesto Sauce, which is stirred into soup by guests.

⊖ *When basil is at its peak, blend up several batches of pesto to freeze. Leave out the cheese which you can add when you use the sauce. Freeze some of your pesto in ice cube trays and pop the frozen squares into a plastic bag in the freezer. You'll have just the right amount to flavor soups and sauces.*

Green Garden Vegetable Soup with Pesto

erves 10 to 12

3	pounds zucchini, sliced
1	large onion, sliced
4	tablespoons butter or margarine
6	cups chicken broth
1	10–ounce package frozen lima beans
1	10–ounce package frozen asparagus
1	10–ounce package frozen peas
1	tablespoon Worcestershire sauce
	salt and pepper
	pesto

Sauté onion and zucchini in butter in a large pot until soft, about 10 minutes. Add chicken broth. Bring to a boil.

Stir in frozen vegetables. Simmer, uncovered, for 20 to 30 minutes. Purée in batches in food processor or blender. Return to pan. Add salt, pepper and Worcestershire sauce. Thin with chicken broth to desired consistency.

Swirl *Pesto Sauce into each cup just before serving.

❧ *Pesto is only considered to have been corrrectly made if the basil leaves were taken from a plant which was in flower.*

Smoothy Soup

Serves 6

	butter or oil
1	medium yellow onion, chopped
2	celery stalks, chopped
1	17–ounce can cream style corn
6	ounces chicken broth
½	cup half and half
	salt and pepper

Sauté onions and celery until translucent.

Purée ingredients in blender. Add seasonings to taste.

Serve hot or cold.

Tomato Bisque

Yield 2 quarts

Excellent served as a first course or as a light lunch!

4	cups fresh tomatoes, quartered
1	cup celery, chopped
½	cup white onion, chopped
4	teaspoons light brown sugar
8	tablespoons butter or margarine
6–8	tablespoons flour
4	cups whole milk
1	large yellow onion
6–8	whole cloves
3	small bay leaves.
	fresh basil, parsley or chives, chopped
	whipped cream
	nutmeg

Preheat oven to 350°.

Simmer tomatoes, celery, chopped onion and brown sugar in covered saucepan for 20 minutes.

Melt butter or margarine in top of double boiler. Add flour and blend with wire whisk. Add milk. Whisk until sauce is thickened and smooth.

Transfer the roux to an ovenproof dish. Stud the onion with whole cloves. Add onion, cloves and bay leaves. Place the dish in preheated oven. Cook slowly for 20 minutes.

Strain tomato mixture through a Foley food mill or press through a colander. Add cream sauce. Blend thoroughly and season as desired.

Serve warm with parsley or basil as garnish. May be served chilled with chopped chives or a dollop of whipped cream with grating of nutmeg.

Bisques are thick, rich soups consisting of puréed seafood, fowl or vegetables and usually heavy cream.

Light Tomato Soup

3	cups homemade defatted chicken or turkey broth
	or
	low fat canned broth
1	medium onion, finely chopped
4	celery stalks and tops, finely chopped
1	teaspoon salt
2	tablespoons brown sugar
2	tablespoons vinegar
1	bay leaf
1	stick cinnamon
6	whole cloves
5	allspice berries
2	cups tomato juice

Sauté onion and celery in their own juice until soft. Add all other ingredients except tomato juice. Simmer for 30 minutes.

Add tomato juice. Heat to boiling. Strain soup and serve hot or cold.

Cream of Pear Soup

2	tablespoons butter
1	large onion, chopped
4	large ripe pears, peeled and chopped
1½	cups chicken broth
	salt and pepper to taste
	crème fraîche
2	thick cut smoked bacon slices, chopped and sautéed
	Italian parsley, chopped

Sauté onion in butter for 5 minutes. Add pears and continue to sauté until juices are released. Add chicken broth. Simmer for 5 minutes.

Purée in blender and return to heat. Add salt and pepper as needed.

Garnish with crème fraîche, bacon and parsley.

☙ *The Comice pear is chubby and green and ranks #1 for eating. It is sweet, juicy and buttery all in one.*

Wild Rice Mushroom Soup

Serves 8 to 12

This is a Minnesota favorite!

5	tablespoons butter
2	medium onions, minced
2	garlic cloves, minced
1	pound mushrooms, sliced
1	cup sherry
1	tablespoon thyme or more to taste
3	cans beef bouillon
1	pound wild rice, cooked
1½	quarts buttermilk
2	tablespoons Maggi seasoning, optional
	salt and pepper to taste

Sauté onions and garlic in butter until limp. Add mushrooms. Sauté 3 minutes. Add sherry and thyme. Simmer 3 minutes.

Add wild rice. Stir and add remaining ingredients. Season to taste and stir.

Simmer 10 minutes.

Cream of Chicken Soup

Serves 6 to 8

1	can cream style corn
1	can cream of chicken soup
1	can chicken and rice soup
2	cups milk
3	bacon slices
1	tablespoon onion, diced
5	tablespoons celery, diced
	almonds, slivered
	parsley, chopped

Heat cream style corn. Put through sieve. Add soups and milk.

Fry bacon, reserving fat. Remove bacon to paper towel and crumble.

Sauté onion and celery in bacon fat. Add to soup mixture and heat.

Serve with crumbled bacon, almonds and parsley sprinkled on top.

❸ *Only the pure in heart can make a good soup.*

—*Ludwig van Beethoven*

Prudy's Great Borscht

Serves 10

5	pounds chuck roast
3	marrow bones
1	large onion, thickly sliced
4	carrots
3	celery stalks
1	tablespoon salt
	ground black pepper, to taste
	parsley
	fresh dill
1	large can tomatoes
4–5	tablespoons fresh lemon juice
2	tablespoons brown sugar
3	garlic cloves, minced
3	jars Harvard beets
3–4	cups cabbage, chopped
	sour cream

First Day: Brown chuck roast on all sides in a large pot. Add marrow bones. Cover with water and boil. Skim foam from surface. Add onion, carrots, celery, parsley, salt, black pepper and lots of fresh dill. Simmer for 2 hours and refrigerate overnight.

Second Day: Remove fat. Pick meat into bite sized pieces. Strain broth. Add tomatoes, lemon juice, brown sugar and garlic. Simmer for 1 hour. Add Harvard beets and cabbage. Simmer for 5 minutes. Top with sour cream when ready to serve.

Cold Cucumber Soup

Serves 6 to 8

Pretty and refreshing!

5	cucumbers
1½	cups parsley, chopped
6	scallions, sliced
2	tablespoons fresh dill, chopped
	or
1	tablespoon dried dill
¼	cup fresh lemon juice
1	quart buttermilk
	freshly ground pepper to taste
	sliced radishes for garnish
	mint leaves for garnish

Peel, chop, salt and drain cucumbers.

Put all ingredients, except radishes and mint, in blender. Blend until smooth and chill well.

Ladle into chilled cups and garnish with radishes and mint leaves.

Curried Shrimp Bisque

Yield 20 cups

A souper supper!

2–3	tablespoons vegetable oil
4	garlic cloves, chopped
5	cups Granny Smith apples, peeled and chopped
3	cups onion, chopped
1	cup carrot, peeled and chopped
1	cup celery, chopped
2	cups red bell pepper, chopped
5	cups chicken broth
3	cups potato, peeled and diced
2	tablespoons curry powder
¾	teaspoon lemon thyme
¾	teaspoon ground cardamom
½	teaspoon ground allspice
2	cups beef stock
1¼	cups instant non–fat milk
2	tablespoons tomato paste
3	cups milk
2	pounds shrimp, cooked and at room temperature
	pepper to taste
	fresh lemon wedges
	parsley or cilantro, chopped

Heat oil in large soup kettle. Add apples, garlic, onions, carrots, celery and red peppers. Sauté until soft and tender.

Add chicken stock, potatoes, curry powder, cardamom, allspice and lemon thyme. Bring to a boil. Reduce heat to simmer. Cover and cook gently until potatoes are tender, 10 to 15 minutes.

Cool mixture slightly and purée in batches. Return purée to soup kettle.

Mix ½ cup beef stock with instant milk powder and the tomato paste. Purée this mixture. Combine with ingredients in kettle.

Add remaining 1½ cups beef stock and milk. Heat all together. Add shrimp and heat through, 3 to 5 minutes. Add pepper to taste.

Garnish with fresh parlsey or cilantro. Pass fresh lemon wedges at the table for individual seasoning.

Black Bean Soup

Serves 3 to 4

This is a delicious soup, especially when made with smoked ham shanks!

1½	cups dried black beans
1½	quarts water
	ham bone or smoked ham shanks
3	celery stalks, chopped
2	medium onions, diced
	bouquet garni
1½	teaspoons black pepper, freshly ground
	salt to taste
¼	cup Madeira wine or juice of 2 lemons

Soak beans overnight. Drain. Put in kettle and add water, ham bone or shanks, celery, onion, bouquet garni and pepper. Cover kettle. Bring to a boil. Simmer for 3 hours or until beans are very tender.

Remove meat from bones and set aside. Discard bones and bouquet garni. Work bean mixture through a sieve or food mill or purée in food processor. Return bean purée and meat to kettle. Add a little more water if soup is very thick. Bring to a boil.

Add Madeira or lemon juice. Taste for seasonings. Serve by itself or with steamed rice added to each bowl.

Split Pea Soup

This is so simple, wonderful and healthy! Freezes beautifully.

1	leftover ham bone
	or
2–3	cracked ham shanks
1–2	bags split green or yellow peas or lentils
2	onions, chopped
10	whole cloves or ½ teaspoon ground cloves
10	peppercorns or ½ teaspoon pepper, freshly ground
½	cup dry sherry
3–5	quarts cold water
	salt and pepper to taste

Cover all ingredients with cold water in large soup pot. Bring to a simmer slowly. Remove any foam that appears. Turn down heat. Simmer soup slowly for 3 to 4 hours until peas are no longer solid.

Remove bones, ham, onion pieces and other solids. Serve as is or purée in blender for a smooth soup.

Lentil and Brown Rice Soup

Serves 8 to 10

Hearty and freezes well!

5	cups chicken broth
2	cups water
1½	cups lentils, rinsed
1	cup brown rice
1	2–pound can tomatoes, chopped
3	carrots, halved lengthwise and sliced ¼ inch thick
1	onion, chopped
1	celery stalk, chopped
3	garlic cloves, minced
½	teaspoon dried basil
¼	teaspoon dried thyme
1	bay leaf
½	cup parsley, minced
1	tablespoon cider vinegar
1	cup red wine
	salt and pepper to taste
	sour cream or plain yogurt
	fresh dill

Combine broth, water, lentils, rice, tomatoes and juice, carrots, onions, celery, garlic, basil, oregano, thyme and bay leaf. Bring to a boil. Cover and simmer for 45 to 55 minutes or until lentils and rice are tender. Stir occasionally.

Stir in parsley and vinegar. Taste for seasoning. Remove bay leaf. Add wine, salt and pepper. Purée half and combine with remaining soup. Serve with sour cream or yogurt and chopped dill.

Zuppa di Fagioli alla Toscana (Tuscan Bean Soup)

Serves 8

½	pound small dried white beans
2	tablespoons olive oil
1	garlic clove, minced
1	tablespoon fresh parsley, chopped
1	celery stalk, finely chopped
¼	teaspoon black pepper, freshly ground
2	quarts water
1	cup tomato sauce
1	teaspoon salt

Soak beans overnight. Put oil, garlic, parsley, celery and pepper in large pot. Sauté until barely brown.

Add beans, water, tomato sauce and salt. Simmer for 2 hours. Mash half of the bean mixture and combine with the unmashed portion. Add salt and pepper if needed. Serve.

Sopa de Tortilla

Serves 6 to 8

1	onion, chopped
1	jalapeño pepper, chopped
2	garlic cloves, minced
	olive oil for sautéing
1	14½–ounce can stewed tomatoes
4	cups stock, chicken or beef
1	can tomato soup
1	teaspoon chili powder
1	teaspoon cumin
½	teaspoon lemon pepper
1	teaspoon Worcestershire
	salt and pepper to taste
2	cups chicken, cooked and shredded
4	corn tortillas, torn into bite-sized strips
2	tablespoons olive oil
1	avocado, cubed
1	cup Monterey Jack cheese, grated
1	large tomato, peeled and diced
	sour cream, optional

Sauté onion, jalapeño pepper and garlic in oil for several minutes. Add stewed tomatoes, stock, soup and seasonings. Cover and simmer for 1 hour.

Sauté tortilla strips in olive oil.

About 10 minutes before serving, add tortilla strips, chicken and tomatoes to soup.

Place cubed avocado and grated cheese in individual bowls. Ladle hot soup on top. Top with sour cream.

Curried Cream Cheese Soup

Serves 4

2	cups beef consommé
4	3–ounce packages cream cheese
¾	teaspoon curry powder
½	garlic clove
	salt and pepper to taste
	chopped chives

Blend first 4 ingredients. Season. Chill until very cold.

Pour into chilled cups, sprinkle with chives and serve.

Pasta, Grains & Vegetarian Dishes

Rice was born in water and must die in wine.

—Old Italian Proverb

Vegetable Lasagna

Serves 8

10	whole wheat lasagna noodles
2	tablespoons olive oil, divided
2	pounds spinach
½	pound mushrooms, sliced
2	medium carrots, grated
1	medium onion, chopped
2	garlic cloves, minced
15	ounces tomato sauce
12	ounces tomato paste
1½	teaspoons dried oregano
1	teaspoon dried basil
3	cups ricotta cheese
2	eggs
4	cups Monterey Jack cheese, grated
	or
2	cups Mozzarella cheese and 2 cups Monterey Jack cheese, grated
1	cup Parmesan cheese, freshly grated

Preheat oven to 375°.

Add lasagna noodles to large pan of boiling water. Reduce heat and simmer until tender, about 7 minutes. Drain. Mix 2 teaspoons oil with the noodles and set aside.

Rinse spinach well. Cook spinach in covered saucepan without water, except for drops clinging to leaves. Reduce heat when steam appears. Cook 3 to 5 minutes. Drain and chop.

Heat remaining oil in large saucepan. Add mushrooms, carrots, onion and garlic. Cook until tender, not brown. Stir in tomato sauce, tomato paste, oregano and basil.

Beat eggs into ricotta cheese in small bowl. Beat until smooth.

Oil 13 x 9–inch ovenproof casserole. Place a layer of half the noodles, then half of ricotta cheese mixture, spinach, Monterey Jack cheese and sauce. Repeat the layers.

Bake for 30 to 40 minutes. Sprinkle with half of the Parmesan cheese. Let stand for 10 minutes before slicing. Serve with remaining Parmesan cheese.

⊖ *Mozzarella is a soft white cheese with a mild, delicate flavor. It originated in southern Italy, where it is still made from water buffalo's milk. Fresh buffalo mozzarella can be found in specialty shops and some supermarkets.*

Spanish Bulgar

Serves 4 to 6

This superb dish may be made in advance and reheated.

	vegetable oil spray
2	carrots, shredded
1	cup mushrooms, sliced
½	green bell pepper, chopped
1	small onion, chopped
1	garlic clove, minced
¼	cup water
1	14–ounce can tomatoes with juice, unsalted
1¼	cups bulgar
2	cups water
1	15–ounce can kidney beans, drained and rinsed
1½	teaspoons chili powder
½	teaspoon thyme
½	teaspoon pepper

Spray medium skillet with vegetable oil. Add carrots, mushrooms, green bell pepper, onion and garlic. Sauté over medium–high heat until vegetables begin to soften. Add water and cook until tender, about 5 minutes. Set aside.

Pour tomatoes and juice into medium saucepan. Insert kitchen shears and cut tomatoes into quarters. Add bulgar and 2 cups of water. Bring to boil over high heat. Reduce heat to medium. Cover and cook 5 minutes.

Add kidney beans, chili powder, thyme and pepper to bulgar and tomatoes. Cover and simmer 10 minutes.

Stir in sautéed vegetables and serve.

Vary recipe by adding other vegetables such as chopped celery or red bell pepper. Use other herbs, such as basil or oregano. Stir in cubes of firm tofu or cooked chicken to vary the dish further.

Bulgar, a nutritious staple in the Middle East, consists of kernels that have been dried and crushed. It is often confused with, but is not the same, as cracked wheat.

Chickpea Vegetable Stew

Serves 4

1	cup chickpeas or garbanzo beans
1	teaspoon salt
2	tablespoons olive oil
1	cup onion, chopped
1	bunch broccoli, chopped
1	cup carrots, julienned
1	pound fresh mushrooms, chopped
2	tablespoons fresh lemon juice
½	cup currants or raisins, optional
	black pepper and cayenne pepper to taste
¼	teaspoon paprika
2	cups millet
3	cups water
1	teaspoon salt
1½	cups cashews, toasted and chopped

Soak chickpeas overnight. Drain. Cook in 4 to 5 cups salted water for 1½ to 2 hours. Will yield 2 cups.

Sauté onion in oil in heavy pan over medium heat until tender, about 5 minutes.

Add carrots, mushrooms, broccoli and lemon juice. Stir and cook until just done, about 8 minutes. Cover with lid to finish.

Add drained chickpeas, raisins and seasonings. Simmer, covered, until heated through.

Cook millet in salted water for 20 minutes.

Serve stew over millet. Sprinkle with cashews.

Cottage Cheese Pancakes

Serves 2

2	eggs or 4 egg whites
1	cup cottage cheese
	or
1	cup ricotta cheese plus 2 tablespoons milk
2	tablespoons wheat germ
2	tablespoons whole wheat flour
	safflower oil or margarine

Combine ingredients in food processor or blender. Blend until smooth, scraping walls of container frequently.

Pour batter onto a heated, lightly oiled griddle forming 4–inch rounds. Cook over medium heat until bubbles form on the surface. Turn and bake other side.

Turkish Bulgar Pilaf

Serves 6 to 8

To cut calories and fat, eliminate pine nuts. It's still excellent!

1½	cups shallots, minced
1	fennel bulb, finely chopped
1	teaspoon salt
1	tablespoon fresh dill
2	tablespoons olive oil
2	cups raw bulgar
2½	cups boiling water
½	cup dried currants
1	cup dried apricots, sliced
1	cup pine nuts, toasted
½	cup parsley, minced

In saucepan, sauté onion, fennel, salt and dill in oil until vegetables are tender.

Add raw bulgar. Sauté over medium heat until bulgar is browned, about 5 minutes.

Add water, currants and apricots. Cover. Simmer for 25 minutes until bulgar is tender and water is absorbed.

Mix in pine nuts and parsley just before serving.

Black Bean Chili

Serves 4

1	tablespoon olive oil
1	cup onion, chopped
2	garlic cloves, crushed
1	28–ounce can whole tomatoes, drained and chopped
2	cups cooked black beans
1	15–ounce can tomato sauce
1	tablespoon chili powder or to taste
1	tablespoon brown sugar
1	tablespoon ground cumin
2	teaspoons dried oregano
½	teaspoon ground coriander
¼	teaspoon allspice
	hot cooked rice

Sauté onion and garlic in olive oil until soft. Add tomatoes, beans, tomato sauce, sugar and spices. Mix well and simmer for 30 minutes. Adjust seasonings.

Serve with hot cooked rice.

Black Bean Tamale Pie

Serves 4

Filling:

1	tablespoon oil
½	cup onion, chopped
½	cup green pepper, chopped
1½-2	cups black or adzuki beans, cooked
1	cup tomato sauce
½	teaspoon chili powder
½	teaspoon cumin
	cayenne to taste

Crust:

1	cup cornmeal
2	teaspoons sugar
½	teaspoon salt
⅓	cup milk
1	egg, slightly beaten
2	tablespoons oil
1	cup corn kernels
1	cup cheese, grated
	kefir or sour half and half, optional
	salsa

Sauté onion and green pepper in oil. Stir in beans, tomato sauce and seasonings.

Combine crust ingredients. Press into 9–inch pie plate. Spoon filling on top. Bake at 350° for 25 minutes.

Sprinkle cheese on top. Bake 5 minutes until cheese is bubbly or put under broiler to brown.

Serve with kefir and salsa.

☙ *For fluffier rice, add one teaspoon of lemon juice to each quart of water while cooking.*

Scrambled Tofu

Serves 4

Trust us and try this! It is best prepared and served immediately.

10	ounces firm tofu, drained
1	tablespoon safflower oil
1	garlic clove, minced
½	green bell pepper, chopped
6	mushrooms, sliced
1	scallion, chopped
1	medium tomato, cut in ½–inch cubes
2	teaspoons soy sauce, low sodium
2	tablespoons fresh parsley, chopped
½	teaspoon dried basil
½	teaspoon dried oregano
	pepper

Mash tofu in a small bowl. Set aside.

Heat oil in a medium–sized skillet over medium–high heat. Sauté garlic, green pepper, mushrooms and scallion. Reduce heat to medium. Stir in tomato, soy sauce, parsley, basil, oregano, pepper and tofu. Stir lightly for about 3 minutes to heat through. Serve immediately.

Vary the recipe by substituting fresh chives for the scallion. Add other vegetables such as shredded carrots, small broccoli florets or zucchini, sliced. Try other herbs such as chili powder, rosemary, sage, thyme or dill. Add 2 eggs or 4 egg whites, lightly beaten, to the tofu. Try topping the tofu with Parmesan cheese, grated, just before serving.

Mock Cheese Soufflé

Serves 3

4	slices bakery white bread, crusts removed
½	pound sharp Cheddar cheese, grated
2	eggs, beaten
1¼	cups milk
½	teaspoon salt
½	teaspoon dry mustard
	green onions or chives, chopped

Break bread into irregular pieces about ½ inch in size. Combine with cheese.

Combine eggs, milk, salt, mustard and onions. Pour mixture over the bread and cheese. Mix well. Place in buttered 1–quart pan. Cover and refrigerate overnight.

Remove from refrigerator ½ hour before baking. Ripple top with fork to make uneven. Bake at 300°, uncovered, until golden brown, about 1½ hours.

This recipe is easily doubled.

Tofu–Stuffed Shells

Serves 4

This entire recipe may be prepared a day ahead. Cover and refrigerate to bake later.

16	large pasta shells
1	tablespoon safflower or olive oil
1	small onion, chopped
2	garlic cloves, minced
1	pound firm tofu, mashed
	or
	low fat ricotta cheese
2	eggs or 3 egg whites, lightly beaten
½	cup grated Parmesan cheese, divided
1	teaspoon basil
½	teaspoon black pepper

Sauce:

1	tablespoon safflower or olive oil
1	small onion, chopped
2	garlic cloves, minced
½	pound mushrooms, sliced
1	medium carrot, shredded
1	celery stalk, finely chopped
2	tablespoons fresh parsley, chopped
1	teaspoon oregano
½	teaspoon basil
¼	teaspoon black pepper
4	8–ounce cans unsalted tomato sauce

Preheat oven to 350°.

Add pasta shells slowly to a large pot of boiling water. Stir to separate. Boil 8 to 10 minutes or until tender. Drain and rinse with warm water. Set aside.

Heat oil in medium skillet. Sauté onion and garlic. Remove from heat. Stir in tofu, eggs, ¼ cup Parmesan cheese, basil and pepper.

Stuff cooked pasta shells with tofu mixture.

Heat oil in medium skillet. Sauté onion, garlic and mushrooms until softened. Add carrot, celery, parsley, oregano, basil, black pepper and tomato sauce. Cover and simmer for 10 minutes.

Pour half of sauce into 11 x 13–inch baking pan. Arrange a single layer of stuffed shells on sauce. Pour remaining sauce over shells. Sprinkle with remaining Parmesan cheese.

Bake for about 30 minutes until hot and bubbling. Let stand 5 minutes before serving.

Vary the recipe by adding 1 to 2 cups shredded spinach to the tofu filling mixture.

White Smash

erves 6

12	flour tortillas
	oil
12	ounces Monterey Jack cheese, chopped finger-sized
1	jalapeño pepper, seeded and chopped
¼-½	cup picante sauce
3	tablespoons butter
3	tablespoons flour
1	cup milk
	garlic powder
	sour cream

Heat oil in skillet. Dip tortilla into heated oil to soften. Drain.

Place 2 cheese fingers, dash of chopped pepper and 1 tablespoon picante sauce on each tortilla. Roll up and place in a row in 8 x 12–inch greased baking dish.

Make white sauce with butter, flour and milk, adding garlic powder to taste. Pour over tortillas.

Bake at 350° for 20 minutes until brown and bubbly. Garnish with sour cream and more picante sauce.

May be prepared a day ahead and refrigerated. Return to room temperature before baking.

Tofu-Nut Pancakes

Serves 2

2	eggs or 4 egg whites
¼	cup cottage cheese
½	cup firm tofu, drained
2	tablespoons milk
2	tablespoons whole wheat flour
1	tablespoon almonds, finely chopped
1	tablespoon wheat germ
¼	teaspoon baking soda
	dash of ground nutmeg
	safflower oil or margarine
2	tablespoons poppy seeds, optional

Combine eggs, cottage cheese, tofu, milk, flour, almonds, wheat germ, baking soda and nutmeg in blender or food processor. Blend well. Add more milk if batter is too thick.

Oil and heat a griddle. Spoon on batter. Cook over medium heat until bubbles rise and begin to break. Sprinkle each pancake with poppy seeds. Turn and cook other side.

Baked Noodles Antin

Serves 6

For a refreshing change, top with mixture of lemon and orange zest. Put under broiler to brown!

5	ounces fine or medium egg noodles
1	cup cottage cheese
1	cup sour cream
1	small onion, finely grated
1	tablespoon Worcestershire sauce
	dash Tabasco
	dash salt

Garnishes:
   paprika
   sour cream
        or
   Parmesan cheese, grated

Cook noodles in boiling salt water until al dente, about 10 minutes. Drain.

Mix other ingredients together. Toss lightly with noodles. Place in buttered 1½ to 2–quart casserole. Cover. Bake at 350° for 45 minutes or until brown.

Serve piping hot with desired garnish.

Microwave Risotto

Serves 4

1½	tablespoons unsalted butter
1½	tablespoons olive oil
⅓	cup shallots, minced
1	cup rice, preferably Arborio
3	cups chicken broth, simmering
¼	cup Parmesan cheese, freshly grated
	additional Parmesan cheese for serving

In a microwave dish, heat butter and oil at full–power for 1 minute. Oven should be at least 500 watts. Stir in shallots. Cook at full–power for 2 minutes. Add rice. Cook at full–power for 2 minutes.

Add broth. Cook, uncovered, at full–power for 6 minutes. Stir well. Continue cooking at full–power for 7 minutes. Remove from oven. Let stand, stirring frequently, until rice absorbs liquid.

Stir in ¼ cup cheese and serve immediately. Pass additional cheese at the table.

Risotto with Fennel

Serves 4

6	tablespoons butter, divided
½	cup yellow onion, chopped
1	1-pound fennel bulb, trimmed, cored, quartered and cut into ¼-inch slices
¼	teaspoon salt
	pinch fresh nutmeg
5	cups chicken stock or broth
1½	cups Arborio rice
¼	teaspoon pepper
¼	cup Parmesan cheese, grated

Melt 3 tablespoons butter in large saucepan. Cook onion over low heat, until onion is soft but not brown, about 3 minutes. Stir in fennel. Season with salt and nutmeg. Mix well. Cover and simmer, about 5 minutes, stirring occasionally.

Add rice to fennel, stirring to coat.

Bring stock to simmer in another pan. Add stock to rice mixture, cup by cup, stirring constantly, until rice absorbs liquid, about 20 minutes. If stock is absorbed before the rice is tender, add hot water. Rice should be moist, but not soupy.

Transfer to buttered casserole. Stir in pepper, Parmesan and remaining butter. Cover with foil. Hold at room temperature until ready to bake. Bake at 350° for 30 to 40 minutes, until heated through and bubbly. Do not overcook.

Wild Rice Casserole

Serves 8

An outstanding accompaniment to poultry, meat, game or fish.

½	pound mushrooms, sliced
1	cup wild rice, washed
6	tablespoons butter
1	small onion, chopped
½	cup almonds, slivered
¼	cup green pepper, chopped
½	cup celery, chopped
	pepper to taste
3	cups chicken stock
2	tablespoons soy sauce

Sauté mushrooms, rice, onion, almonds, pepper and celery in butter in heavy saucepan, for about 5 minutes.

Transfer to casserole. Add stock, soy sauce and pepper. Cover tightly.

Bake at 325° for 2 hours.

Aromatic Rice Pilaf

Serves 8

4	cups water
4	cloves
1	cinnamon stick
⅛	teaspoon powdered saffron
4	chicken bouillon cubes
¼	cup butter
2	cups converted rice
½	cup almonds, slivered
¼	cup golden raisins
¼	cup currants
1	tablespoon butter

Combine first 5 ingredients in saucepan. Bring to boil. Turn off heat and steep for 20 minutes.

Sauté rice in ¼ cup butter until well coated and slightly translucent. Add the aromatic bouillon. Cover tightly. Simmer 15 to 18 minutes or until all liquid is absorbed.

Sauté almonds, raisins and currants in remaining butter until almonds are slightly browned. Stir almond mixture into rice.

Pack hot rice into a buttered 6–cup mold. Invert on serving platter and serve.

Gnocchi alla Romana

Serves 6

6	cups cold water
2	teaspoons salt
1	cup farina
	dash cayenne pepper
3	tablespoons butter
⅓	cup Parmesan cheese, grated
	melted butter
	additional Parmesan cheese, grated

Bring water and salt to rolling boil. Reduce to simmer and let farina trickle in, stirring constantly. Keep mixture smooth. Remove from heat. Stir in cayenne, butter and ⅓ cup Parmesan.

Rinse jelly roll pan with cold water. Spread mixture evenly on it with rubber spatula. Cool. Cover with wax paper and refrigerate until set, about 30 minutes. Remove pan from refrigerator. Cut circles from cold, firm farina with 2–inch biscuit cutter or cut 1½–inch squares with sharp knife.

Brush bottom of large au gratin dish with melted butter. Arrange rounds or squares of gnocchi in one layer, overlapping, in dish. Brush with melted butter and sprinkle with Parmesan. Brown under hot broiler.

New Orleans Red Beans and Rice

Serves 8 to 10

1	pound dried red beans
1	pound salt pork
1	large onion, chopped
1	cup green onions, chopped
½	cup green pepper, chopped
2	garlic cloves, minced
2	bay leaves
	juice of ½ lemon
	salt and pepper to taste
	few dashes Tabasco sauce
	zest of ½ lemon

Cover beans with water. Soak overnight. Drain.

Cover again with water. Add salt pork, onion, peppers, garlic and bay leaves. Bring to a boil. Reduce heat and simmer for 3 to 4 hours, stirring occasionally. Remove salt pork and bay leaves when beans become creamy.

Add lemon juice. Cook 1 hour, stirring frequently. Watch closely to prevent burning. Season to taste with salt, pepper and Tabasco.

Serve over steamed rice. Top with lemon zest.

Curried Beans and Rice

Serves 4

A terrific vegetarian dish!

2	tablespoons oil
1	cup onion, minced
2	garlic cloves, minced
¾	cup carrots, diced
½	cup zucchini, diced
1	tablespoon lemon juice
1	tablespoon honey
2	teaspoons curry powder
2½	cups cooked brown rice
1	cup small red beans, cooked
	salt and pepper to taste

Sauté onion in oil for 5 minutes in large skillet. Use medium-high heat. Add garlic, carrots and zucchini. Cook 5 minutes. Add lemon juice, honey and curry. Cook 1 to 2 minutes. Remove from heat.

Stir in cooked beans and rice. Season to taste. Transfer to lightly greased, 1½ to 2–quart casserole. Cover.

Bake at 350° for 30 minutes.

Capellini d'Angelo

Serves 4

½	pound angel hair pasta
½	pound Italian sausage, sweet or hot
2	tablespoons oil
1	pound zucchini, julienned
2	tablespoons garlic, minced
½	pound mushrooms, sliced
1	green pepper, coarsely chopped
3	tomatoes, cored and cut into ¼–inch cubes
2	teaspoons Cajun seasonings
1	tablespoon butter
⅓	cup Parmesan cheese, grated

Cook pasta until al dente. Drain.

Brown sausage in large skillet. Remove from pan. Discard drippings.

Sauté zucchini, green pepper and garlic in same pan for 1 minute. Add mushrooms. Sauté for 2 minutes. Stir in tomatoes. Cook 1 minute. Add sausage and pasta to pan. Toss with Cajun seasonings and butter. Remove from heat.

Transfer to serving dish. Sprinkle with cheese and serve.

Fettuccine with Pine Nuts, Prosciutto and Brown Butter

Serves 3

¾	pound fresh
½	cup butter
2	teaspoons fresh lemon juice
2	ounces thinly sliced prosciutto, torn into 2–inch strips
1	cup fresh parsley, finely chopped
⅓	cup pine nuts, toasted lightly

Cook fettuccine in boiling water until al dente. Drain.

Heat butter in skillet over moderate heat. Swirl until it is golden brown. Remove from heat. Stir in lemon juice, prosciutto, parsley and pine nuts.

Toss fettuccine with butter sauce in large bowl. Salt and pepper to taste.

The four pronged fork was invented in Naples at the court of King Ferdinand II in order to eat spaghetti elegantly.

Capellini with Black Pepper and Prosciutto

Serves 4 to 6

¼	cup lemon zest, cut into long, very thin strips
4	tablespoons unsalted butter
2	tablespoons olive oil
2	large garlic cloves, minced
2	large shallots, minced
6	ounces thinly sliced prosciutto, stacked and cut crosswise into ¼-inch strips
¾	pound capellini
1	teaspoon black pepper, coarsely ground
	Parmesan cheese, freshly grated

Blanch the zest strips in a small saucepan of boiling water for 1 minute. Drain and set aside.

Cook garlic and shallots in butter and olive oil until softened, stirring occasionally. Increase heat to medium-high. Add prosciutto and zest. Cook until prosciutto is lightly browned, about 3 minutes.

Cook capellini in boiling water until al dente. Drain well.

Add pasta and black pepper to prosciutto mixture. Toss to combine thoroughly.

Serve hot or at room temperature, with cheese on the side.

Lemon Linguine

Serves 2

1	large yellow onion, chopped
4	tablespoons olive oil
1½	tablespoons lemon juice
	zest from ½ small lemon, slivered
¼	pound linguine
⅓	cup fresh Parmesan cheese, grated
4	tablespoons Italian parsley, coarsely chopped

Cook onion slowly in oil in covered sauté pan, until translucent. Add lemon juice.

Blanch zest several times in boiling water.

Cook and drain linguine. Toss into onions mixture. Toss with cheese. Add more oil if mixture seems dry.

Divide into 2 bowls. Sprinkle with lemon zest and parsley. Serve.

Baked Pasta with Tomatoes, Shiitake Mushrooms and Prosciutto

Serves 6 to 8

Great with a green salad, a fresh loaf of bread and full-bodied Italian red wine!

2	packages dried shiitake mushrooms
2	cups onion, chopped
2	large garlic cloves, minced
¼	teaspoon dried hot pepper flakes
1	teaspoon dried basil, crumbled
1	teaspoon dried oregano, crumbled
2	tablespoons olive oil
4	tablespoons unsalted butter, divided
3	tablespoons all-purpose flour
2	cups milk
1	28-ounce can crushed tomatoes
¼	pound thinly sliced prosciutto, cut into strips
¼	pound Fontina cheese, grated
¼	pound Gorgonzola cheese, crumbled
1½	cups Parmesan cheese, grated, divided
1	pound farfalle (bow tie) pasta

Soak dried mushrooms in water for 30 minutes. Discard stems. Slice caps.

Sauté onion, garlic, pepper flakes, basil and oregano until onion is softened. Add mushrooms. Cook mixture over low heat until mushrooms are tender, about 10 to 15 minutes. Transfer mixture to large bowl.

Melt 3 tablespoons butter in skillet. Whisk in flour. Cook roux, stirring, for 3 minutes. Add milk in steady stream, stirring constantly. Simmer mixture until it is thickened, about 2 minutes.

Pour sauce over mushroom mixture. Add tomatoes, prosciutto, Fontina, Gorgonzola and 1¼ cups of Parmesan. Stir gently until lightly mixed.

Add splash of olive oil to kettle of boiling water. Add pasta. Cook 5 minutes. Pasta will not be fully cooked. Drain well. Add pasta to mushroom mixture. Toss until it is well combined. Transfer to buttered 3 to 4–quart baking dish.

Pasta may be prepared to this point and kept covered and chilled overnight. Bring pasta to room temperature before baking.

Sprinkle with remaining Parmesan. Dot with remaining butter. Bake in 425° oven for 25 to 30 minutes or until top is golden and pasta is tender.

If possible, prepare this dish a day before serving and chill overnight. The flavors are greatly enhanced.

Very Easy Pasta Sauce

Serves 4

2	tablespoons olive oil
3	tablespoons butter
2	garlic cloves, minced
½	carrot, grated
½	small onion, chopped
1	teaspoon thyme
1	tablespoon Italian seasoning
½	teaspoon pepper, freshly ground
1	teaspoon salt
½	cup green or black olives, chopped
5	small Roma tomatoes, chopped
8	ounces tomato sauce
1	pint heavy whipping cream
	corkscrew pasta
	Parmesan or Romano cheese, freshly grated

Melt butter in oil. Sauté garlic, carrot and onion. Do not brown. Add seasonings, olives, tomatoes and tomato sauce. Stir.

Add cream and bring just to boil. Reduce heat to medium and cook for 10 minutes.

Serve over pasta, topping with cheese.

Pasta Germaine

Can be done weeks in advance.

Sauce:

2	pounds ripe tomatoes, peeled, seeded and diced
6	tablespoons extra virgin olive oil
1	tablespoon fresh oregano
2	tablespoons Italian parsley, chopped
1	large garlic clove, minced
3	tablespoons Romano or Parmesan cheese, freshly grated
	salt to taste
	freshly ground pepper
1	pound fresh spaghetti, cooked

Blend sauce ingredients well, letting them rest for at least 1 hour before serving. <u>Do not cook.</u>

Pour a little sauce on plate. Serve noodles. Pour sauce on top of noodles.

Linguine with Broccoli in Sweet Tomato Sauce

Serves 4

A colorful and delicious low–fat and low–sodium entrée.

4	cups broccoli florets
1	tablespoon olive oil
2	garlic cloves, minced
4	large ripe tomatoes, peeled, cored and chopped
	or
1	28–ounce can low–sodium tomatoes, chopped, with juice
2	tablespoons golden raisins, chopped
½	cup pine nuts, toasted
6	ounces linguine
2	tablespoons parsley, chopped

Cook broccoli in enough unsalted, boiling water to cover just until tender. Rinse under cold water, drain and set aside.

Heat olive oil in a large saucepan. Sauté garlic in heated oil for 3 minutes or until golden. Add tomatoes, raisins and cayenne. Simmer for 15 minutes, uncovered. Add pine nuts and simmer 5 minutes.

Cook linguine according to package directions, omitting salt. Drain well and place in large pasta bowl that has been warmed.

Add broccoli to warm tomato sauce. Toss to heat through. Pour over pasta and sprinkle with parsley.

White Clam Sauce for Pasta

Serves 4

3	tablespoons olive oil, divided
2	garlic cloves, crushed
½	pound fresh mushrooms, cleaned and chopped
	or
6	anchovy fillets, chopped
2	6½-ounce cans minced clams
¼	cup parsley, minced
	salt and freshly ground pepper to taste

Sauté garlic in 2 tablespoons olive oil until lightly browned.

Sauté mushrooms in 1 tablespoon olive oil. Combine with garlic. Add clams with liquid. Heat to simmer, but do not boil. Correct seasonings. Add parsley just before serving.

Serve over hot, cooked pasta.

Pasta Creations On-the-Run

Select your favorite fresh pasta and top with one of the following sauces.

Pasta with Bleu Cheese

Heat chicken broth. Dissolve 1 cube of chicken bouillon in it. Add cream and Italian bleu cheese. Warm until cheese is melted.

Pasta with Garlic

Sauté minced garlic in olive oil. Add additional olive oil. Heat. Stir into pasta. Top with fresh, chopped herbs.

Pasta with Vegetables

Sauté bouquet of fresh vegetables in olive oil. Add to pasta. Top with grated Parmesan cheese.

Pasta with Scallops

Sauté scallops in reduced fish stock. Add cream. Pour over pasta and sprinkle with chopped dill.

Pasta with Oriental Turkey

Sauté turkey in reduced chicken broth. Add white wine and shredded ginger. Pour over pasta. Sprinkle with chopped cilantro.

 You can tell if raw fresh pasta is of good quality from the way it looks. It should be shiny and deep yellow.

EDOUARD VUILLARD

Place St. Augustin, 1912–13

Bequest of Putnam Dana McMillan

Coiled Basket, Apache, 19th–20th century
The Ethel Morrison Van Derlip Fund

Manufactured by Minton
Game Pie Dish, English, 1877
The David Draper Dayton Fund

PIETER CLAESZ.
Still Life, 1643
The Eldridge C. Cooke Fund

Fish & Seafood

Glory be to God for dappled things. . .
For rose—moles all in stipple upon trout that swim.

—Gerald Manley Hopkins

Oven–Poached Fillet of Salmon

Serves 4

1	fillet of salmon, about 1½ pounds, skinned
1	lemon, very thinly sliced
2	teaspoons dill weed
2	tablespoons butter
¼	teaspoon salt
⅛	teaspoon pepper
1	tablespoon capers
2	tablespoons parsley, chopped

Preheat oven to 350°.

Place piece of foil, large enough to wrap fillet, on a cookie sheet or roasting pan. Place fillet in center. Top with lemon slices and dot with butter. Sprinkle with dill, salt and pepper. Close foil tightly.

Place in preheated oven. Bake 30 to 40 minutes, until flaky.

Serve with capers and chopped parsley.

Grilled Salmon with Sweet Onion Relish

Serves 4

4	salmon steaks
2	large sweet onions, Walla Walla or Vidalia
¼	cup olive oil
1	tablespoon sugar
1	bay leaf
1	sprig fresh thyme
1	tablespoon balsamic vinegar

Grill salmon steaks 12 to 15 minutes, depending on thickness.

Sauté onions in olive oil until transparent. Add sugar and herbs. Cook until mixture is caramelized. Add vinegar to taste.

Serve sauce over grilled salmon steaks.

 To remove fish and onion odors from hands, wash hands in salted water or rub with a piece of lemon dipped in salt.

Salmon Baked in Foil

Serves 8 to 10

1	6-8 pound salmon, cleaned
1	cup carrots, sliced
1	cup onion, sliced
1	cup celery, sliced
½	teaspoon thyme
	salt to taste
8	peppercorns, crushed
1	garlic clove, crushed
1	bay leaf
2	cups dry white wine

Preheat oven to 400°.

Place cleaned salmon in center of baking sheet covered with a long piece of foil. Add carrot, onion, celery, thyme, salt, peppercorns, garlic, bay leaf and wine. Seal foil tightly around salmon.

Bake for 50 minutes to 1 hour. When fin can be removed easily, the fish is done. Remove from oven and cool.

When cool, skin and bone.

Serve warm or chilled with hollandaise or sauce of your choice.

Herbed Salmon Steaks

Serves 8

8	salmon steaks, 1-inch thick
¼	cup butter, melted
2	tablespoons fresh tarragon or 2 teaspoons dried
1	cup fresh lemon juice
2	tablespoons shallots, finely chopped
1	teaspoon pepper, freshly ground

Combine butter, tarragon, lemon juice, shallots and pepper. Mix well.

Place salmon steaks on rack on broiler pan. Brush with several tablespoons of sauce.

Broil 6 inches from heat for about 7 minutes. Turn steaks and brush with more sauce. Broil 5 more minutes or until fish is flaky.

Serve with remaining sauce.

Swordfish with Red Pepper Hollandaise

Serves 4

4	swordfish steaks

Marinade:

2	tablespoons olive oil
2	tablespoons fresh lemon juice
2	medium garlic cloves, minced
1	medium shallot, minced

Red Pepper Hollandaise:

1	large red pepper
3	egg yolks
2	tablespoons fresh lemon juice
½	teaspoon salt
	pinch white pepper
	pinch cayenne pepper
½	cup unsalted butter

Combine marinade ingredients and pour over fish. Marinate at least 1–2 hours, turning a couple of times.

Roast pepper in 500° oven until blackened. Peel skin from pepper, cut open, remove seeds and drain on paper towel.

Place in food processor or blender fitted with steel blade. Purée, remove and set aside.

In a food processor or blender, combine egg yolks, lemon juice, salt, white pepper and cayenne. Blend for 10 seconds.

Heat butter until sizzling, but not browned. Slowly pour butter into blender or food processor with motor running. Add red pepper purée and taste for seasoning.

Grill or broil fish 3 inches from source of heat, about 4 to 5 minutes per side.

Place swordfish on plate and spoon hollandaise sauce over fish.

 We urge our readers to consider the possible danger of serving eggs that have not been completely cooked.

Red Snapper à la Vera Cruzana

6	red snapper fillets
	juice of 1 lemon
2	onions, sliced in rounds
2	garlic cloves, minced
¼	cup olive oil
3	tomatoes, peeled and chopped
1	tablespoon lime juice
⅛	teaspoon ground cloves
⅛	teaspoon cinnamon
⅛	teaspoon each salt and ground pepper
3	jalapeño peppers, cut into strips
½	cup pimento–stuffed olives, sliced
¼	cup capers

Sprinkle snapper with lemon juice and set aside.

Sauté onions and garlic in olive oil in heavy skillet until tender, but not brown. Add tomatoes, lime juice, cloves, cinnamon, salt and pepper. Simmer for 5 minutes until consistency of heavy cream.

Sauté snapper for 2 minutes on each side. Transfer to serving dish. Cover with the sauce and garnish with peppers, olives and capers.

Ginger Grilled Swordfish

6	swordfish steaks, 1–inch thick
1	tablespoon fresh ginger, grated
1	teaspoon black pepper, freshly ground
½	cup fresh cilantro
1	garlic clove
¼	cup soy sauce
¼	cup olive oil
	juice and zest of 2 lemons

Combine all ingredients, except swordfish, in a food processor and purée. Pour into covered bowl and refrigerate for at least 6 hours or overnight.

Place fish in large baking pan 1 hour before grilling. Cover with marinade, turning fish to coat.

Grill fish on oiled grill over medium hot coals. Cook for 5 to 6 minutes on each side, basting with marinade, until lightly browned.

Baked or Broiled Fish with Asparagus Sauce

Serves 4

1	pound asparagus stalks
3	garlic cloves
½	small onion
2	cups chicken stock
1	tablespoon parsley
2	ounces heavy cream
	salt and pepper to taste
	dash of Tabasco
	dash of lemon juice
4–6	fish fillets, skinned

Use tender center of asparagus stalks and tips. Steam ½ of tips until just tender and set aside for garnish.

Place asparagus stalks, remaining tips, garlic and onion in saucepan. Cover with chicken stock and simmer until tender. Add parsley and remove from heat.

Place in blender and add cream while blending. Remove and add other seasonings, adjusting to taste. Keep warm.

Season your choice of white fish with salt and pepper.

Broil for about 5 minutes with margarine, white wine or a little water to prevent sticking, or bake at 425° for 8 to 10 minutes.

Serve sauce over fish, using steamed asparagus tips for garnish.

Tuna Steaks with Rosemary Butter

Serves 6

6	tuna steaks
	rosemary sprigs for garnish

Marinade:

½	cup olive oil
¼	teaspoon pepper
2	tablespoons fresh ginger, minced
4	tablespoons soy sauce

Rosemary Butter:

½	stick butter
1	tablespoon black olives, chopped
¼	teaspoon Dijon mustard
2	teaspoons fresh rosemary, chopped

Marinate steaks for 30 minutes.

Grill 4 minutes per side. Serve hot with dab of rosemary butter. Garnish with rosemary sprig.

Shrimp Chinoise

Step One:

1	pound buckwheat noodles
2	tablespoons sesame oil
3	tablespoons scallions, sliced thinly
2	tablespoons peanut oil
1	tablespoon hot chili oil
3½	tablespoons soy sauce
1½	tablespoons balsamic vinegar
1	tablespoon sugar
	salt to taste

Step Two:

2	tablespoons rice wine vinegar
1	tablespoon cider vinegar
1	tablespoon chili oil
2	tablespoons soy sauce
½	cup sesame oil
1	cup vegetable oil
2	garlic cloves, minced
	juice of 1 lemon
1	teaspoon Dijon mustard
1	tablespoon honey
2	pounds shrimp, cooked

radicchio or red flowering kale
sesame seeds
red bell pepper, cut into fine strips

Step One:

Cook noodles in lightly salted water for about 10 minutes or until tender. Drain and rinse in cold water. Drain again. Toss with sesame oil. Let sit.

Mix other ingredients in step one together. Pour over noodles and toss. Let stand 1 hour.

Step Two:

Combine all ingredients in step two. Toss with cooked shrimp. Let stand at least 1 hour.

Line serving bowl with radicchio or red flowering kale. Add noodles. Top with shrimp mixture. Sprinkle sesame seeds over top.

Garnish with fresh red pepper strips.

Shrimp à la Grecque

Serves 4

¼	cup olive oil
½	cup onion, chopped
1	16–ounce can stewed tomatoes
4	medium tomatoes, peeled and chopped
1	cup dry white wine
1	bay leaf
1	teaspoon dried oregano, crushed
1	teaspoon sugar
1	tablespoon Worcestershire sauce
½	pound Feta cheese
1½	pounds raw, medium shrimp
	parsley

Fry onions in olive oil until soft, 5-10 minutes, in a non-corrosive Dutch oven or kettle.

Squeeze juice out of canned tomatoes. Add to onions. Squeeze juice out of fresh tomatoes. Add fresh tomatoes, wine, bay leaf, oregano, sugar and Worcestershire to the mixture. Simmer gently for 20 minutes. Season to taste with salt and pepper.

Add Feta cheese and simmer 5 more minutes. Thicken sauce slightly with cornstarch, if necessary. Add shrimp and cook until pink and tender. Add parsley.

Serve with rice pilaf.

Sauce may be cooked in the morning, adding cheese, shrimp and parsley just before serving.

Salmon Pizza

Serves 4 to 6

1	large Boboli pizza crust
1	cup prepared Alfredo sauce
1	4 ½–ounce package Morey's Alaskan Smoked Salmon
½	cup green onions, sliced
1	2¼–ounce can sliced black olives
	or
½	cup green olives, sliced
1	8–ounce package Italian style shredded cheese

Preheat oven to 400°.

Spread Alfredo sauce over the crust. Cut salmon into small cubes. Layer over sauce with onions and olives. Top with cheese.

Bake for 10 minutes or until cheese bubbles.

Scallops with Lemon Parsley Sauce

Serves 4

This is equally good with cubes of swordfish or fresh tuna.

3	tablespoons butter
3	tablespoons olive oil, more if needed
1¼	pounds fresh scallops
3	garlic cloves, chopped
1½	cups bottled clam juice
⅔	cup white wine or chicken stock
½	teaspoon dried red pepper, crushed
1	lemon rind, grated
2	tablespoons lemon juice, freshly squeezed
12	ounces fresh pasta
½	cup parsley, chopped
	salt and freshly ground pepper to taste

Melt butter and oil in large frying pan. Add scallops and sauté for 2 minutes, turning to coat all sides. Remove from pan and set aside.

Add garlic to butter and oil in pan, adding a small amount of olive oil if necessary. Sauté 1 minute. Add clam juice, wine or stock and red pepper. Boil until mixture is reduced to 1¼ cups, about 10 minutes. Add scallops, lemon rind and lemon juice. Simmer until scallops are cooked through.

Cook pasta in boiling water until barely tender, about 2 minutes. Drain pasta and add to frying pan. Add parsley. Toss until pasta is well coated with sauce. Add salt and pepper to taste.

Serve on warmed plates with a salad and crusty French bread to complete the meal.

Keith's Pizza with Shrimp and Pesto

Serves 4 to 6

Innovate to your heart's desire.

1	pizza crust in tube, refrigerator section
½	cup pesto sauce
4–6	Roma tomatoes
12	ounces shrimp, medium or small
1	12–ounce package mozzarella slices
	Feta cheese, crumbled

Bake pizza crust according to directions. Do not brown.

Spread pesto sauce on baked crust. Slice tomatoes and place on crust. Add shrimp and top with mozzarella. Sprinkle with Feta.

Return to oven until heated through and cheese is melted.

Shrimp with Vermicelli

Serves 8

1	pound shrimp, peeled and deveined
4	garlic cloves, minced
2½	tablespoons olive oil
1½	pounds pea pods
1	bunch asparagus, cut into 1–inch pieces
3-4	scallions, chopped
1	pound vermicelli
1	7–ounce jar sun–dried tomatoes
6	ounces Montrachet cheese
¼	cup pine nuts
½	cup Parmesan cheese, grated
¼	cup pesto

Sauté shrimp and garlic in olive oil just until shrimp are pink. Remove shrimp from pan or wok. Stir–fry pea pods, asparagus and scallions until crisp and tender.

Cook vermicelli.

Add shrimp back to vegetables. Add the next 5 ingredients. Heat and toss with the vermicelli.

Serve hot or at room temperature.

Scallops with Sweet Red Pepper and Snow Peas

Serves 4

Serve over pasta or rice.

½	pound snow peas
4	tablespoons olive oil
4	tablespoons shallots, minced
1	sweet red pepper, julienned
1	pound scallops
2	tablespoons fresh lemon juice
4	tablespoons fresh basil, coarsely chopped
⅓	teaspoon red pepper flakes
	salt and pepper to taste

Blanch snow peas 30 seconds in boiling water. Set aside.

Sauté shallots in olive oil, about 1 minute. Add red pepper strips and sauté for 2 to 3 minutes. Add scallops, lemon juice, basil, salt and pepper. Cook about 2 minutes, stirring constantly.

Add snow peas and cook until all are heated thoroughly, about 1 minute. Do not overcook. Serve immediately.

Scallops with Mushrooms and Tomatoes

1½	pounds bay scallops
¼	cup olive oil
4	tablespoons unsalted butter
	flour for dusting
3	tablespoons shallots, minced
¾	pound mushrooms, sliced
½	teaspoon thyme
½	teaspoon basil
	salt and pepper to taste
½	cup white wine
1	cup tomatoes, peeled, seeded and chopped
1	garlic clove, minced
2	tablespoons fresh parsley, chopped
	juice of 1 lemon

Heat 3 tablespoons oil and 1 tablespoon butter over moderate heat. Dust scallops with flour, shaking off excess. Sauté for 3 to 4 minutes. Transfer to a bowl.

Add remaining 1 tablespoon oil and 3 tablespoons butter to skillet and cook shallots, stirring for 1 minute. Add mushrooms, thyme, basil, salt and pepper. Cook 2 to 3 minutes or until mushrooms begin to give off liquid. Add wine and reduce to half.

Stir in tomatoes and any accumulated juices from the bowl of scallops. Reduce the liquid, stirring, until thick. Stir in the scallops and garlic. Cook mixture, stirring, until scallops are heated through. Add parsley and lemon juice.

Serve over wild rice or in patty shells.

Quick–Fix Parmesan Fish

Serves 3 to 4

No–fail microwave.

1	pound mild white fish
¼	teaspoon seasoned salt
2	tablespoons butter or margarine
½	cup Parmesan cheese, grated
½	cup mayonnaise
2	tablespoons green onions, chopped
	paprika

Rinse and dry fish. Arrange in 9 x 13–inch baking dish. Sprinkle with seasoned salt. Dot with butter. Cover with waxed paper and microwave on high for 2 minutes.

Blend cheese, mayonnaise and onions. Spread mixture over fish and cover with waxed paper. Microwave on high for 2–3 minutes or finish under pre–heated broiler until cooked through and lightly browned.

Sprinkle with paprika and serve.

Dorothy's Shrimp Supper Dish

Serves 8

Excellent for brunch, luncheon or light supper!

For deviled eggs:

3	tablespoons mayonnaise
3	tablespoons butter or margarine, melted
3	teaspoons sweet pickle, chopped
1½	teaspoons vinegar
⅓	teaspoon dry mustard
	dash Worcestershire sauce
	salt and pepper to taste

To assemble:

9	eggs, hard boiled, halved and deviled
1	pound mushrooms, sliced and sautéed
1	pound cooked shrimp
2	cups Cheddar cheese, grated and divided
2	cups thick white sauce

Remove yolks from halved eggs. Mix yolks and remaining ingredients together. Fill egg white halves with yolk mixture and set aside.

Place sautéed mushrooms in bottom of 9 x 13–inch glass baking pan. Place eggs on mushrooms. Scatter shrimp around eggs.

Melt 1½ cups cheese into white sauce. Pour over shrimp, mushrooms and eggs. Sprinkle remaining cheese on top.

Bake at 350° for 30 minutes or until heated through and cheese is melted.

Baked Fillet of Sole

Serves 4 to 6

2	pounds sole fillets
1	stick butter, softened
1	tablespoon white wine vinegar
1	tablespoon Worcestershire
1	tablespoon lemon juice
1	teaspoon Dijon mustard
1	teaspoon salt
½	teaspoon pepper, freshly ground
½	cup breadcrumbs
	paprika

Combine butter, vinegar, Worcestershire, lemon juice, mustard, salt and pepper to make a smooth spread.

Butter an ovenproof casserole or au gratin dish. Sprinkle with breadcrumbs. Spread butter mixture on fillets and place in dish. Sprinkle with paprika.

Bake at 400° for 20 minutes.

Freezer Seafood Newburg

Serves 4

2	cups cooked lobster, crab or shrimp, coarsely chopped
2	tablespoons butter or margarine, melted
1	tablespoon flour
1	tablespoon rice flour
¼	teaspoon salt
¼	teaspoon paprika
	dash cayenne pepper
	dash nutmeg
2	cups light cream or half and half
¼	cup dry sherry, optional
	toasted English muffins
	or
	hot cooked rice
	fresh parsley, chopped

Arrange seafood evenly in four 4½–inch individual foil pans, one 8–inch foil cake pan or freezer–safe 1–quart casserole. Drizzle with melted butter.

Mix flours, salt, paprika, cayenne and nutmeg in small pan. Stir in cream, gradually, to make a smooth mixture. Heat to simmering until thickened and blend in sherry. Pour sauce over seafood and freeze immediately. After frozen, wrap well and store in freezer.

When ready to serve, bake uncovered in 350° oven until sauce is hot and bubbling, about 30 minutes for individual casseroles or 1 hour for large pan. Stir gently to blend sauce and seafood.

Serve over toasted English muffins or cooked rice. Sprinkle with parsley.

❧ *The art of cooking still embraces four of the five senses, giving taste, texture and delight to the nose and to the eye. No other art does that.*

—Samuel Johnson

Meat

The nearer the bone the sweeter the meat.

—Olde English Proverb

Rack of Lamb with Tomato Mint Salsa

Serves 2 per rack

Salsa:
2	large ripe tomatoes, diced
1	small red onion, finely diced
1½	tablespoons fresh mint, chopped
1	teaspoon cilantro, chopped
½	teaspoon salt
⅛	teaspoon pepper
	dash Tabasco
	juice of ½ lime
3	green onions, finely chopped
2	garlic cloves, minced

Lamb:
	rack or loin of lamb, split and chinned
	salt and pepper
	fresh mint leaves
	olive oil

Mix all ingredients for salsa. Allow to stand at least 1 hour. Adjust seasonings, if necessary.

Season lamb well with salt and pepper. Rub with fresh mint leaves and olive oil. Sear in hot skillet, browning all sides. Finish cooking in 425° oven for 15 minutes or until meat thermometer reads 125° to 130°. Remove and let stand several minutes.

Serve with salsa on the side or over the top.

Swedish Leg of Lamb

Serves 8

5–6	pound leg of lamb
	black pepper, freshly ground
3	medium yellow onions, sliced
3	carrots, peeled
½	cup half and half
1½	cups strong coffee, hot
1	tablespoon sugar
1	cup beef broth or bouillon, hot

Preheat oven to 425°.

Pepper meat and place on rack in roasting pan. Put onions and carrots on bottom of pan. Roast for 30 minutes.

Reduce heat to 350°. Add bouillon, cream and sugared coffee. Roast 1 hour, basting 3 times.

Transfer lamb to a platter. Scrape pan and put all contents into blender. Purée for gravy.

The lamb will be pink. Cook an additional 20 minutes for well done lamb.

Loin Lamb Chops with Red Peppers and Mint

Serves 6

2	tablespoons butter
2	tablespoons garlic, minced
4-6	red peppers, seeded and julienned
3	tablespoons fresh mint, chopped
	or
3	tablespoons fresh basil
6-12	loin lamb chops
	salt and pepper, freshly ground
2	tablespoons butter, softened
	whole mint leaves

Sauté 1 tablespoon garlic in butter for 1 minute. Do not brown. Add peppers and 2 tablespoons mint or basil. Cook for 3 to 4 minutes, stirring frequently. Season with salt and pepper to taste. Set aside, but keep warm over low heat.

Season lamb chops with salt and pepper. Grill or broil for 3 to 4 minutes for medium-rare.

Combine butter, remaining mint and remaining tablespoon of garlic to make a smooth paste.

Place 1 or 2 lamb chops on each plate. Surround with peppers. Garnish each chop with teaspoon of mint butter and fresh mint leaves.

Ragoût of Lamb

Serves 4

1½	pounds lean lamb, preferably from leg
2	tablespoons flour
	salt and pepper to taste
1	cup consommé
	chopped parsley for garnish
3	tablespoons olive oil
¼	cup sherry
1	clove garlic, minced
1	tablespoon lemon or lime juice

Cut lamb into 1½-inch cubes. Dredge in mixture of flour, salt and pepper.

Heat oil in large skillet and brown meat. Add remaining ingredients except juice. Bring to boil. Pour into a casserole and cover.

Bake in 350° oven for 1 to 1½ hours or until lamb is done, but not dry. Add more consommé, if necessary. Add lemon or lime juice.

Serve at once over saffron rice. Sprinkle chopped parsley generously over the lamb.

Lamb Curry

This dish may be made ahead and reheated before serving.

4	pounds leg of lamb, cut into 1–inch pieces
2	tablespoons oil
2	tablespoons butter
2	tablespoons curry
1	garlic clove, pressed
3	medium onions, chopped
2	celery stalks, chopped
2	tart apples, chopped
1	tomato, chopped
1	small eggplant, pared and cut into ½–inch chunks
2	cups condensed chicken broth
2	teaspoons salt
2	tablespoons brown sugar
	rind of 2 lemons, grated
½	cup yogurt

Condiments:

¾	cup shredded coconut, toasted
½	cup green onions, chopped
4	dill cucumber pickles, diced
½	cup dark raisins, steamed until plump
½	pound bacon, diced and cooked until crisp
	Major Grey's chutney

Brown lamb in oil and butter. Stir in curry and continue cooking for 2 minutes. Add garlic, onions, celery, apples, tomato and eggplant. Heat through. Add chicken broth, salt, brown sugar and lemon rind. Stir in yogurt.

Lower temperature and simmer 45 minutes. Transfer lamb to heated serving dish.

Place condiments in separate bowls and serve.

☻ *A garlic tip: Blend 10–12 heads in food processor. Roll processed garlic in plastic wrap in shape of a log. Wrap again in foil and freeze. Cut off slice when needed.*

California Curried Lamb

2	cooking apples, cored, pared and sliced
1	green pepper, chopped
2	onions, sliced
1	garlic clove, minced
	olive oil
2	tablespoons flour
1	tablespoon curry powder
½	teaspoon salt
½	teaspoon marjoram
½	teaspoon thyme
1	can consommé
½	cup dry red wine
	juice of 1 lemon
	zest of 1 lemon
2	whole cloves
3	cups cooked leg of lamb, diced
1	tablespoon sour cream

Sauté apples, onions and pepper in olive oil in large skillet until onions are limp. Sprinkle with flour, curry powder, salt, marjoram and thyme. Mix well and cook for 5 minutes, stirring constantly.

Add consommé, red wine, lemon juice, lemon rind and cloves. Simmer for 20 to 30 minutes. Add lamb and heat for 15 minutes.

Just before serving, mix in sour cream. Serve with fluffy white rice and your favorite condiments.

☙ *Curry powder may contain a blend of as many as twenty herbs and spices; among those most frequently used are cardamom, cloves, coriander, cumin, ginger and turmeric.*

Posh Pot Roast with Vegetables

Serves 6 to 8

3-4	pound pot roast, your favorite cut
	salt and pepper to taste
	pinch celery seeds
¼	teaspoon oregano
3	tablespoons wine vinegar
1	medium onion, sliced
3-4	potatoes, quartered
3-4	onions, quartered
2	celery stalks, 2–inch slices
5-6	carrots, thickly sliced

Trim pot roast of any fat. Place under broiler. Brown meat on both sides. Season with salt and pepper.

Place browned meat in casserole or Dutch oven. Add celery seeds, oregano, vinegar and sliced onion. Cover tightly and simmer over low heat 3½ hours. Turn occasionally. Casserole may be refrigerated overnight and fat skimmed, if desired.

Add vegetables to casserole. Cover. Simmer for 1 hour.

Remove meat and vegetables to heated platter. Serve with pan juices, thickened or not as desired.

Belgian Beef Stew

Serves 4

Wonderful for a casual, winter supper that can be prepared ahead.

2	pounds boneless chuck, cut into 2–inch cubes
	flour
	salt and pepper
2	tablespoons bacon fat
3	large onions, chopped
1	large carrot, chopped
1	12–ounce bottle dark beer
	water
1	tablespoon wine vinegar
3	sprigs thyme
1	bay leaf, crumbled
	salt and pepper to taste
2	tablespoons brown sugar

Dust the meat with seasoned flour. Heat fat in heavy casserole and sauté beef. Add onions and carrot. Cook until brown. Add beer and enough water to cover. Add vinegar, thyme, bay leaf, salt and pepper to taste. Bring to boil. Reduce heat and simmer for 2 hours or until meat is tender. Add brown sugar and simmer for 15 minutes.

Serve with boiled potatoes, a crusty baguette and salad.

Aprés Ski Supper

erves 6 to 8

erfect mid–winter supper
rved with a salad and bread

1	cup lentils, well rinsed
3	tablespoons vegetable oil
2	onions, chopped
4	garlic cloves, minced
2	28–ounce cans plum tomatoes, drained and chopped
2	pounds Polish sausage or kielbasa, cut into ½ inch slices
1	teaspoon sugar
½	teaspoon pepper
2	bay leaves
	salt

Put lentils into Dutch oven with enough salted water to cover. Bring to boil. Cover and cook over low heat until lentils are tender, but still hold shape. Drain and reserve liquid.

Heat vegetable oil in the same pan. Add onions and garlic. Sauté until onions are tender, but not browned. Add tomatoes and cook until liquid has evaporated. Add sausage and toss the mixture. Add lentils, sugar, salt, pepper and bay leaves. Stir in lentil liquid.

Bake at 350° for 30 minutes.

May be prepared the day before serving. Bring casserole to room temperature before baking.

Italian Lamb Stew

erves 4 to 6

A wonderful fall dinner or
prés ski supper for family
nd friends.

3–4	pounds lamb for stew, cut into serving pieces
3	tablespoons olive oil
2–3	leeks, cut into strips
8–10	garlic cloves, minced
1	can whole tomatoes, reserve liquid
1	small can tomato purée
2–3	cups chicken stock and liquid from can of tomatoes
	salt and pepper to taste
	thyme or rosemary
1	green pepper, cut into strips
	chopped parsley
	rice or pasta

Brown meat in olive oil. Add leeks and garlic. Cook a few minutes, while stirring. Add tomatoes, all liquids and tomato paste. Sprinkle with salt, pepper, thyme or rosemary and simmer for 15 minutes.

Add green pepper. Boil until meat is tender. Sprinkle with lots of parsley.

Serve with rice or pasta.

Meatloaf with Chicken and Pistachios

Serves 12

Good fare for an elegant picnic!

2	pounds meatloaf mixture, beef, veal and pork
2	eggs
¾	cup broth
¾	cup dry bread crumbs
⅓	cup onions, minced
1	garlic clove, minced
½	teaspoon Tabasco sauce
1	large chicken breast, boned, skinned and cut into strips
2	teaspoons lemon peel, ground
¼	cup fresh parsley, chopped
½	cup pistachios, shelled
	watercress
	cherry tomatoes
	hot mustard, optional

Combine meatloaf mixture, eggs, broth, bread crumbs, onions, garlic and Tabasco in bowl. Pat ½ of mixture into a 9 x 5–inch loaf pan. Sprinkle half of nuts over meatloaf mixture.

Toss chicken strips with lemon peel and parsley. Press chicken strips and remaining nuts into meat mixture. Cover with remaining meatloaf mixture.

Bake at 350° for 50 minutes or until meat thermometer reaches 160°. Cover loaf with waxed paper and 2–pound weight to remove air bubbles. Refrigerate overnight.

Serve chilled or at room temperature. Slice thinly and serve on bed of watercress with hot mustard. Garnish with cherry tomatoes.

Can be frozen up to 3 months.

Mushroom Meat Loaf

Serves 4

1	pound mushrooms, chopped
1	pound extra lean ground beef
1	medium onion, chopped
1	cup soft bread crumbs
2	eggs, slightly beaten
1	teaspoon salt
¼	teaspoon pepper
½	cup chili sauce, optional
2	strips of bacon, optional

Mix together all ingredients except chili sauce and bacon. Place in 8 x 4–inch loaf pan. Spread mixture with chili sauce and bacon strips.

Bake at 350° for 1 hour.

Danish Meatballs

½	pound boneless veal
½	pound boneless pork
1	medium onion
3	tablespoons flour
½	cup club soda
1	egg, well beaten
1	teaspoon salt
	fresh parsley, chopped
¼	teaspoon pepper
4	tablespoons butter
2	tablespoons vegetable oil

Combine veal, pork and onion in a food processor. Add flour. Gradually add soda and blend until light and fluffy. Beat in egg, salt and pepper. Cover and refrigerate 1 hour.

Shape into oval patties 4 inches long, 2 inches wide and 1 inch thick. Heat butter and oil to high heat in skillet. Add meat without crowding. Cook 6 to 8 minutes on each side. Remove to warm platter.

Serve with red cabbage.

Skillet Sirloin

2	pounds sirloin, ground
2	eggs
1	garlic clove, minced
½	cup sour cream
2	tablespoons celery leaves, chopped
	thyme, paprika, and salt to taste
1–2	red onions, sliced
1–2	green peppers, chopped

Bring meat to room temperature. Work eggs into meat.

Mix garlic into sour cream. Add celery leaves, thyme, paprika and salt. Add to meat and mix well.

Form meat mixture into a flat cake to fit into an electric frying pan. Leave a trench around the outside. Meat should be 2 to 3 inches thick. Cover with onions and green peppers.

Cook at 250° for 5 minutes. Lower temperature and simmer for 30 minutes. Baste meat every 10 minutes with juices that collect in trench.

Serve with pasta.

Sliced Barbecued Beef for Sandwiches

Fills 36 buns

6	pound beef rump roast

Marinade:

¼	cup cider vinegar
½	cup water
¼	cup sugar
4	teaspoons prepared mustard
1	teaspoon pepper, freshly ground
1	teaspoon salt
2	lemons, sliced

Sauce:

2	medium onions, sliced
½	cup butter or margarine
1	cup ketchup
3	tablespoons Worcestershire sauce

Roast beef to desired doneness.

Combine ingredients for marinade in a pan and simmer for 1 hour. Slice roasted beef in thin slices. Combine the sliced beef and marinade. Refrigerate overnight.

Sauté onions in butter until transparent. Add ketchup and Worcestershire. Combine beef with sauce and heat before serving.

Fill each bun with a few warm slices.

Broiled Flank Steak

Serves 4

2	pounds flank steak

Marinade:

3	tablespoons scallions, minced
1½	tablespoons soy sauce
2	tablespoons olive oil
¾	teaspoon Italian herb seasoning
5	drops Tabasco
3	tablespoons fresh lemon juice
2	teaspoons fresh rosemary

Make marinade in a 12 x 14 glass dish. Place flank steak in dish and marinate at least ½ hour to all day, turning occasionally.

Broil steak 3 to 4 minutes on each side for medium rare.

Slice against grain into very thin slices.

Cold Peppered Tenderloin with Creamy Tarragon Caper Sauce

Serves 4

1½ to 2	pound beef tenderloin, at room temperature, trimmed and tied
1	tablespoon black pepper, coarsely ground
1	teaspoon coarse salt
2	tablespoons vegetable oil

Sauce:

1	egg yolk
2	tablespoons heavy cream
2	tablespoons white wine vinegar
1	teaspoon Worcestershire sauce
1½	teaspoons Dijon mustard
½	cup olive oil
1½	teaspoons fresh tarragon, minced
1	tablespoon capers, drained
2	tablespoons scallions, minced
2	tablespoons fresh parsley, minced
	salt to taste

Preheat oven to 500°.

Pat tenderloin dry and coat all sides with pepper and salt. Place tenderloin in an ovenproof skillet just large enough to hold the meat. Heat the oil over high heat until hot, but not smoking. Brown tenderloin on all sides.

Roast tenderloin for 15 to 20 minutes or until meat thermometer registers 130°. Let cool to room temperature.

Blend the yolk, cream, vinegar, Worcestershire sauce and mustard in blender or food processor. Add oil slowly in a stream with motor running until the mixture is emulsified. Transfer mixture to small bowl and stir in tarragon, capers, scallions, parsley and salt.

Slice the tenderloin crosswise into ⅓ inch slices. Arrange slices on a platter and spoon the sauce over the meat.

If you grow your own tarragon, it's easy to harvest it in the fall and dry it for later use. Remember to pick the tarragon sprigs before the day heats up.

Salpicon (Mexican Shredded Beef)

Serves 16 to 20

This is a perfect dish for a buffet table.

8	pounds top sirloin or eye of round
2	garlic cloves
1	bay leaf
1	12–ounce can tomatoes
¼	cup fresh cilantro, diced
	salt and pepper to taste
1	8–ounce bottle Italian salad dressing
	or
8	ounces vinaigrette with Italian herbs
1	cup garbanzo beans
1	cup green chilies, chopped
½	pound Monterey Jack cheese, cut into ½ inch squares
2	avocados, cut into strips
1	bunch parsley

Place beef in heavy pot and cover with water. Add garlic, bay leaf, tomatoes, cilantro, salt and pepper. Cook over medium heat about 5 hours. Remove meat from broth. Cut into 2–inch squares. Shred and arrange in 9 x 11–inch dish. Cover beef with vinaigrette.

Marinate in refrigerator overnight.

Arrange beans, chilies, cheese and avocados in layers over the beef before serving. Decorate with parsley.

Saltimbocca alla Romana

Serves 4

4	veal steaks for scaloppine
16	sage leaves, fresh
4	slices prosciutto
2	tablespoons butter
1	teaspoon lemon juice
1	tablespoon brandy
½	cup dry white wine

Pound veal steaks until very thin. Put 4 sage leaves on each steak. Cover with prosciutto. Thread with 6–inch skewer.

Sauté in butter about 4 minutes on each side. Add lemon juice and brandy and heat a few minutes.

Place veal on hot serving platter. Add wine to lemon–brandy mixture and reduce briefly. Pour sauce over veal and serve.

Veal Chops with Mushroom Sauce

Serves 4

4	veal chops, thick cut
1	ounce dried porcini or morel mushrooms, chopped
1	cup water
2	tablespoons olive oil
2	tablespoons onion, minced
2	tablespoons carrot, minced
2	tablespoons celery, minced
½	teaspoon salt
¼	teaspoon pepper
1	cup tomato sauce, preferably fresh
½	cup prosciutto ham, shredded
1½	tablespoons capers, chopped

Soak mushrooms in water for ½ hour. Drain and set aside.

Sauté vegetables in olive oil for 10 minutes, stirring occasionally. Add the mushrooms, salt and pepper. Cook for 5 minutes, stirring frequently. Add tomato sauce, ham and capers. Cook for 25 minutes.

Serve over grilled veal chops.

Veal Dijon

Serves 4 to 6

1	small leg of veal, boned and rolled, about 2¾ pounds
½	cup butter, melted
1	8–ounce jar Dijon mustard
¼	cup sherry
1	10½–ounce can consommé
	arrowroot flour, dissolved
	parsley, chopped

Preheat oven to 300°.

Place meat in shallow roasting pan. Blend butter and mustard and pour over meat, covering all sides. Roast 4 hours. Baste at least 3 times during the last hour with mixture of sherry and consommé.

Make gravy of pan juices, thickening with arrowroot. Sprinkle chopped parsley over gravy.

Allow meat to cool for 15 to 20 minutes for easier carving.

Herbed Loin of Pork

Serves 6–8

Putting the vegetables under the roast acts as a rack and flavors the meat and drippings.

6	pound pork loin roast
3	teaspoons salt
1	teaspoon black pepper
1	teaspoon thyme
½	teaspoon nutmeg
1	large onion, quartered
2	carrots, quartered
2	whole cloves
1	garlic clove, crushed
2	celery stalks
1	bay leaf
1¼	cups dry white wine, divided
1¼	cups bouillon, divided
½	cup water
1	lemon

Mix salt, pepper, thyme and nutmeg. Rub onto roast several hours in advance. Make a bed for the meat with the vegetables, cloves, bay leaf and garlic. Set roast on vegetable bed and pour ½ cup of wine and ½ cup stock over the meat. Roast at 475° for 20 minutes.

Reduce heat to 350° and continue baking, 20 minutes per pound, basting with pan juices, adding water if necessary.

Remove roast to platter. Squeeze lemon over the meat. Skim fat from roasting pan. Add remaining wine and stock. Add water. Boil rapidly, scraping the pan. Reduce to 1 cup.

Slice and serve.

Pork Chops and Rice

Serves 4

An old family favorite.

4	loin pork chops
¾	cup long grain rice
2	10½–ounce cans consommé
1	medium onion, sliced
	parsley, chopped

Spray large skillet with non–stick oil. Brown chops on both sides. Remove chops. Add rice and consommé to pan. Stir well.

Place chops on top of rice. Cover chops with onion slices.

Cover pan and cook over low heat until liquid is absorbed by rice, about 35 minutes. Garnish with parsley.

Lamb Shanks

Serves 4

4	lamb shanks
1	garlic clove
1	large onion, thinly sliced
2	cups white wine
2	16-ounce cans stewed tomatoes
2	teaspoons dried dill weed or more if desired
1	teaspoon dried oregano or more if desired
2	teaspoons dried rosemary or more if desired
¼	teaspoon dried thyme or more if desired
½	cup brown sugar, packed
2½	teaspoons salt
¼	teaspoon pepper
1	can tomato bisque soup

Place shanks with other ingredients in covered roaster. Bake at 300° for about 2 hours. Remove cover and bake 30 minutes longer. Remove lamb to serving platter and set aside.

Pour pan juices into saucepan and add tomato bisque soup. Reduce by half over high heat, stirring frequently.

Pour sauce over meat and serve.

Medallions of Pork with Raspberry Sauce

Serves 4 to 6

2	tenderloins of pork
2	tablespoons butter
2	tablespoons canola oil
1	cup fresh or frozen raspberries
2	tablespoons red currant jelly
	or
	port wine jelly
2	tablespoons Framboise liqueur
2	tablespoons heavy cream

Slice tenderloin into ½ inch thick medallions. Heat butter and oil in medium skillet and sauté pork until slightly pink. Remove medallions to heated serving platter and keep warm.

Deglaze pan with Framboise.

Add raspberries and jelly to pan juices. Stir until jelly melts and berries are mushy and put through sieve to remove seeds. Add cream to sauce to thicken. Reheat sauce until just warm through and pour over pork.

Garnish with fresh raspberries and serve.

Pork Roast with Pears

Serves 10 to 12

2	2¼–pound boneless pork roasts
8	garlic cloves, slivered
2	tablespoons candied ginger, slivered
2	tablespoons dried rosemary
	salt and pepper
6	cups pears, peeled, cored and sliced into eighths
2	tablespoons butter
6	tablespoons red currant jelly
4	tablespoons soy sauce
4	tablespoons red wine vinegar
1	teaspoon cayenne pepper
½	cup red wine

Pierce pork at intervals and insert garlic and ginger slivers. Rub with rosemary, salt and pepper.

Sauté pears in butter until soft. Remove pears. Deglaze pan with red wine. Add remaining ingredients. Reduce for 10 minutes on medium–high. Add pears and keep warm.

Roast pork in 350° oven for approximately 1 hour or until temperature reaches 130°–140°. Serve pork with pears around sides.

Grilled Pork Tenderloin

Serves 4 to 6

¾	cup vegetable oil
¼	cup dry white wine
4	garlic cloves, minced
1½	pounds pork tenderloin, trimmed

Mustard Sauce:

¾	cup dry white wine
2	tablespoons shallots, minced
1	cup heavy cream
3	tablespoons Dijon mustard
	freshly ground white pepper to taste

Combine oil, wine and garlic in small deep dish large enough to hold pork. Add pork and marinate in refrigerator overnight. Drain pork and grill on oiled rack for 25 minutes or until meat thermometer registers 155°. Cook tenderloin in 2 tablespoons of oil in large skillet if grill is not available. Turn and brown for about 10 to 15 minutes.

In a small saucepan, boil wine and shallots until reduced to about 2 tablespoons. Add cream and bring to boil. Simmer for 2 minutes until slightly thickened. Strain through a sieve. Whisk in mustard, salt and pepper.

Cut pork into diagonal slices. Serve with mustard sauce.

Crown Roast of Pork with Sherry Stuffing

8-10	pound crown roast of pork
	juice of 1 lemon
2	teaspoons garlic powder

Serves 12

Delicious served with
*Prune Sauce.

Preheat oven to 350°.

Have butcher form loins of pork into a crown. Rub pork with lemon juice, sprinkle with garlic powder and season with salt and pepper.

Place pork on a sheet of aluminum foil in baking pan. Cover rib ends with foil to prevent burning.

Bake roast for 2 hours. Fill cavity with warm stuffing. Roast an additional 35 to 40 minutes or until meat thermometer reads 185°.

Sherry Peach Stuffing

Serves 12

1	cup dried peaches
1	cup dry sherry, divided
2	onions, chopped
4	tablespoons unsalted butter
	turkey giblets, ground
6	cups stale bread
2	tablespoons fresh sage
1	teaspoon white pepper, freshly ground

Plump dried peaches in ½ cup sherry.

Cook onions in butter until golden, 3 to 4 minutes. Add giblets and remaining sherry. Simmer 40 minutes or until giblets are cooked through.

Add remaining ingredients. Mix well. If dressing is too dry, add up to 1 cup of chicken broth.

> *As for anything labeled "sherry cooking wine," avoid it!*
> *The real thing is much better. Cooking wines were*
> *invented so that they could be sold without a liquor license*
> *and be used by teetotalers, and some say to keep the chef*
> *from drinking on the job!*

Poultry & Game

Poultry is for the cook what canvas is for the painter.
—Brillat Savarin

Lemon Roasted Chicken with Rosemary

Serves 6

2	3½ to 4–pound whole frying chickens
2	teaspoons *Seasoned Salt for each chicken
2	whole lemons
2	large sprigs fresh rosemary or 2 teaspoons dried rosemary
	string for trussing and tying

Rub about ½ teaspoon *Seasoned Salt into cavity of each chicken.

Pierce lemons many times with skewer. Place 1 lemon and 1 sprig rosemary in cavity of each chicken. Truss chickens and tie legs together.

Rub outer surfaces of chickens with remaining *Seasoned Salt. Place chickens, breast side down, on V-rack in roasting pan over ½ inch water.

Roast chickens at 450° for 30 minutes. Turn breast side up. Roast additional 30 minutes.

Transfer to cutting board. Tent with foil and allow to stand 10 minutes before carving.

Quick Tandoori Chicken

Serves 4

Be sure to have your kitchen exhaust fan on high when you make this.

1½	pounds chicken breasts, boned and skinned
3	tablespoons butter
1	medium onion, thinly sliced, then cut slices in half
4–6	carrots, scraped and sliced into thin rounds
2	garlic cloves, minced
3	heaping teaspoons tandoori powder
6	hard shakes ground turmeric
4	hard shakes ground cloves
7	ounces Chaokoh (coconut milk), including solids and liquid
	salt to taste

Cut chicken into chunks, ¾ inch by 1½ inches.

Melt butter in large, heavy pan with cover. Cook onion, carrot and garlic over medium heat until onions are transparent. Stir several times.

Sprinkle spices over vegetables. Cook over low heat for 5 minutes, stirring several times.

Add chicken. Cook over medium heat for 6 minutes. Stir occasionally. Add coconut milk and salt. Stir until milk is evenly incorporated. Add more liquid if you want more sauce. Cover and cook over low heat for 5 minutes. Adjust salt to taste.

Serve over plain white or basmati rice. Indian Chutney* compliments this dish.

Spiced Raspberry Chicken

	melted butter
2–3	pounds chicken parts
	salt and pepper to taste
¼	cup raspberry preserves
1	tablespoon Dijon mustard
1	tablespoon tarragon vinegar
2	teaspoons lemon juice

Preheat oven to 350°.

Coat bottom of large baking pan with melted butter. Add chicken. Salt and pepper chicken to taste.

Combine raspberry preserves, mustard, tarragon vinegar and lemon juice. Mix well. Pour marinade over chicken.

If boneless chicken parts are used, bake 20 to 25 minutes. If bone–in chicken parts are used, bake 50 minutes.

Day–Before Chicken

4–6	chicken breasts, thighs or combination of both, boned and skinned
4	ribs celery, coarsely chopped
1	large onion, coarsely chopped
1	green pepper, coarsely chopped
1	teaspoon mixed Italian seasonings
½	cup bleu cheese, crumbled
2	cups prepared spaghetti sauce

Place chicken in bottom of baking pan. Layer vegetables over chicken. Sprinkle with Italian seasonings and cheese. Top with spaghetti sauce.

Cover with foil and bake at 350° for 1½ to 2 hours. Refrigerate overnight so flavors blend.

Reheat, covered, at 350° for 30 minutes or until hot.

Serve with pasta, French bread and salad.

For variety, add mushrooms, summer squash, zucchini and red or yellow pepper.

Binky's Cuban Chicken

Serves 6

3	pounds chicken breasts
2	tablespoons olive oil
1	large onion, chopped
2	garlic cloves, chopped
2	15–ounce cans tomatoes
⅔	cup white wine
½	teaspoon cumin
½	teaspoon oregano
1	cup chicken broth
½	cup slivered almonds, toasted
2	tablespoons raisins
2	tablespoons capers
	salt and pepper to taste
3	tablespoons pimento olives, chopped

Brown chicken in olive oil. Add onion and sauté until transparent. Add garlic and tomatoes. Simmer 5 minutes.

Add remaining ingredients except salt, pepper and olives. Cook, covered, for 45 to 60 minutes. Season with salt and pepper.

Sprinkle with olives before serving. Serve with rice.

Poached Chicken Breasts

Serves 4

Very easy and colorful.

2	tablespoons olive oil
2	garlic cloves, minced
2	tomatoes, chopped
2	onions, sliced
½	cup green pepper, chopped
4	mushrooms, sliced
2	whole chicken breasts, split, boned and skinned
4	slices Havarti or Mozzarella cheese
	capers
	parsley or tarragon

Place first 7 ingredients in large skillet. Cover. Cook over low heat for 30 minutes.

Place cheese slices on top of chicken just before serving. Let melt for several minutes.

Sprinkle with capers and parsley or tarragon and serve.

Chicken Cacciatore with Artichokes

6	chicken breast halves, with bone and skin
⅓	cup flour
2	tablespoons olive oil
2	6–ounce jars marinated artichoke hearts, cut in quarters; reserve liquid from one jar
1	16–ounce can of tomatoes, chopped in large pieces; reserve liquid
½	pound mushrooms, thickly sliced
4	garlic cloves, minced
1	teaspoon salt
½	teaspoon oregano
½	cup dry sherry

Preheat oven to 450°.

Dredge chicken in flour and place in large baking pan. Pour olive oil and oil from one jar of artichokes over chicken. Bake for 10 to 15 minutes, turning chicken once. Place tomatoes and mushrooms around chicken.

Blend liquid from tomatoes with garlic and spices in blender. Pour sauce over chicken.

Reduce oven to 350°. Bake chicken for 60 minutes. Remove from oven. Add artichoke hearts and sherry. Bake for additional 10 minutes.

White Meat Loaf

1	pound raw white turkey meat, ground
⅓	pound veal, ground
¼	cup celery, minced
¼	cup onion, minced
¾	cup white bread crumbs
¼	cup milk
1	egg
1	teaspoon salt
½	teaspoon white pepper
1	large garlic clove, minced

Preheat oven to 350°.

Combine all ingredients well. Form into loaf and put into 4 x 8–inch loaf pan.

Bake 1 hour and 15 minutes. Serve hot or cold.

Cumberland sauce complements this nicely.

Chicken in Foil

Serves 4

Wonderful served with fresh vegetables from the garden.

2	cups prepared herb stuffing
1	cup orange juice, freshly squeezed and warmed
2	tablespoons orange zest
½	cup sweet onion or chives, finely chopped
4	pieces aluminum foil, 8 x 10–inches
2	large chicken breasts, split in half
1½	tablespoons butter, melted
	cracked pepper
	orange slices poached briefly in orange juice, drained

Combine stuffing, juice, zest and onion or chives.

Brush foil with melted butter. Place mound of stuffing on each piece of foil. Top with chicken breast half. Brush chicken with remaining butter. Sprinkle with pepper. Form foil pouch to enclose chicken.

Bake 20 minutes at 350°. Open foil and bake additional 10 minutes or until cooked through and browned.

Carefully remove each portion from foil using spatula, separating stuffing from chicken.

To garnish, fan orange slices on each service plate.

Oven Fried Chicken

Serves 4

1	frying chicken, cut into serving sized pieces
1	cup skim milk
½	cup bread crumbs
⅓	cup Parmesan cheese, grated
¼	teaspoon lemon pepper
¼	teaspoon thyme
¼	teaspoon garlic powder
¼	teaspoon parsley flakes

Soak chicken in milk for one hour.

Combine bread crumbs, cheese and spices. Dip chicken in dry mixture. Place in baking pan.

Bake at 375° for 45 minutes.

Oslo Stew

Stew:

1	whole chicken, rinsed
2	10½–ounce cans chicken broth
¾	cup water
1	bay leaf
1	teaspoon savory
5	onions, quartered
5	carrots, quartered
5	celery stalks, cut into 1–inch slices
2	tablespoons flour
2	tablespoons butter or margarine
8	ounces fresh mushrooms, halved
	salt and pepper to taste

Dumplings:

2	cups prepared biscuit mix
1	teaspoon savory
1	teaspoon dill
⅔	cup milk

Place chicken in large stock pot or Dutch oven. Add chicken broth, water, bay leaf and savory. Cover and simmer 1 hour or until chicken is fork tender. Remove chicken from broth. Cool chicken and reserve broth. Add vegetables, except mushrooms, to broth. Simmer for 30 minutes. Remove vegetables from stock and set aside.

Chill stock for several hours or overnight. Skim off fat and discard.

Brown flour in small skillet over medium heat for about 5 minutes, stirring constantly. Add butter or margarine. Cook and stir to make a roux. Slowly add 1 cup of reserved stock to roux, stirring constantly. Return mixture to reserved stock.

Remove skin and bones from chicken and cut meat into chunks. Return chicken and thickened broth to stock pot. Add mushrooms. Heat to bubbling and add salt, pepper and additional savory, if needed.

Mix biscuit mix, savory, dill and milk. Do not over mix. Form 12 dumplings, using spoons, and drop onto bubbling stew. Simmer uncovered for 10 minutes. Cover and cook for 10 more minutes. Serve in deep bowls.

θ *The reasonably priced ingredients for this dish remind us of the traditional frugality of Norwegians. This trait is precisely summed up in the old folk saying "Smuler er ogsaa brod" or "Crumbs are also bread."*

Chicken Valencia

Serves 6

⅔	cup dark and golden raisins
2	tablespoons sherry
2	tablespoons butter, softened
¼	cup ham, chopped
1	tablespoon parsley, chopped
¼	teaspoon orange peel, grated
¼	cup soft stale bread, cubed
6	large chicken breasts, boned
¾	cup flour
1	teaspoon paprika
½	teaspoon garlic salt
3	tablespoons fat
½	cup orange juice
1	cup chicken broth
¼	cup green onions, chopped
1	cinnamon stick, 2 to 3 inches long
	salt and pepper
4	cups cooked rice

Marinate raisins in sherry for 30 minutes. Drain.

Mix ¼ cup of raisins with butter, ham, parsley, orange peel and bread. Place stuffing in center of each chicken breast. Fold over chicken breast and seal with toothpick.

Combine flour, paprika and garlic salt. Dredge each stuffed breast in flour mixture.

Brown both sides of chicken in fat, in large skillet. Drain excess fat. Add orange juice, chicken broth, green onions and cinnamon stick. Salt and pepper to taste. Cover and simmer 30 to 40 minutes until chicken is tender.

Discard cinnamon. Skim off fat.

Add reserved raisins and simmer 3 to 4 minutes. Thicken with cornstarch, if desired.

Serve with combination of white and wild rice.

Marinades, usually a mixture of wine and oil, onions, spices and herbs are useful for flavoring poultry and game. Even the toughest game, after several days in a marinade, becomes tender and succulent. Cook the marinade down to make a sauce for the final presentation.

Crusted Chicken Breast with Jalapeño Roasted Corn Sauce

Serves 6

The sauce is also good with beef.

Sauce:

6	ears fresh corn, husk left on
1	medium onion, coarsely chopped
1	medium carrot, coarsely chopped
¾	red pepper, coarsely chopped
1–2	jalapeño peppers, optional
5	garlic cloves, minced
	chicken stock
3	ounces heavy cream
	salt and pepper to taste

Crust:

1½	cups pecans or walnuts, finely chopped
½	cup bread crumbs
3	eggs
½	cup milk
3	chicken breasts, split, boned and skinned
	flour to dredge chicken breasts

Preheat oven to 400°.

Place ears of corn on baking sheet in oven. Bake approximately 30 to 40 minutes, until husks begin to brown. Remove from oven and allow to cool.

Husk corn. Use sharp knife to remove kernels from ears. Place in stock pot with onion, carrots, peppers and garlic. Cover with chicken stock. Simmer until tender.

Blend vegetables and stock in blender in two batches. Add small amount of heavy cream to each batch to bind and smooth consistency of sauce. Starch in corn will thicken sauce. Add more chicken stock, if sauce is too thick. Salt and pepper to taste.

Mix nuts with bread crumbs. Combine eggs and milk in separate bowl. Season chicken breasts with salt and pepper. Dredge in flour, then in egg mixture and finally, in pecan breading.

Brown chicken breasts on one side in hot skillet. Place in pan, browned side up. Finish in 425° oven for 30 minutes.

Thinly slice chicken breasts and serve on top of sauce for a pleasant presentation.

Waterzooi of Chicken

Serves 4 to 6

2	onions, finely chopped
2	shallots, finely chopped
3	leeks, white only, finely julienned 1 inch long
4	celery stalks, finely julienned 1 inch long
3	carrots, finely julienned 1 inch long
4	parsley roots, finely julienned 1 inch long
4	tablespoons butter
1	large roasting chicken, skinned and cut into 8 pieces
6–8	cups well flavored chicken or veal stock
	salt and white pepper
4	egg yolks
½	cup heavy cream
	juice of one lemon
1	tablespoon parsley, chopped

Stew all the vegetables in large casserole with butter for 20 minutes. Place chicken pieces over vegetables. Cover with stock and season to taste. Cover and bring to a boil. Reduce heat and simmer gently until chicken is cooked, about 30 minutes.

Beat egg yolks and cream together. Add 1 tablespoon of hot liquid from stew to cream mixture. Blend. Add cream mixture gradually to stew. Use very low heat to avoid curdling! Season to taste with lemon juice, salt and pepper.

Top with parsley. Serve with boiled potatoes.

A traditional Belgian dish that makes a wonderful winter meal with crusty French bread and hearty red wine. It is customary to eat potatoes on the side, but they can be added to stew at the table.

The general preference is for white wines with white meated birds and red wines with dark–meated, rich–fleshed birds, such as duck or goose. If the turkey or chicken has a spicy sausage stuffing, consider a red wine with it. Game birds are almost always served with full–bodied red wine.

Chicken with Peanuts

Serves 4

½	cup water
½	cup dry sherry
½	cup soy sauce
2	tablespoons dark corn syrup
1	tablespoon vinegar
4	teaspoons cornstarch
	oil
6	large chicken breasts, boned, skinned and cut into ½–inch cubes
1	cup peanuts, salted or unsalted
½–¾	cup green onions, sliced
3	garlic cloves, minced
½	teaspoon ground ginger
1	teaspoon crushed red pepper

Stir together water, sherry, soy sauce, corn syrup, vinegar and cornstarch. Blend thoroughly and set aside.

Add oil to wok. Stir–fry chicken 2 to 3 minutes until chicken turns white. Make a well in center of chicken. Add peanuts. Stir–fry approximately 30 seconds. Push mixture up sides of wok. Add onions, garlic, ginger and crushed red pepper to middle. Stir–fry 1 minute.

Stir sauce and add to center of wok. Bring to boil without stirring, about 1 minute. Cook additional minute or until thickened, stirring rest of ingredients with sauce.

Serve with white rice.

Persian Chicken

Serves 6

1	chicken, cut into pieces or boneless chicken pieces
	oil or butter
1	large onion, chopped
½	teaspoon nutmeg
½	teaspoon cinnamon or more
1	teaspoon salt
¼	teaspoon pepper
2	cups chicken stock or water
20–25	prunes or dried apricots, tossed in melted butter

Brown chicken in oil or butter. Add onion, nutmeg and cinnamon. Fry briefly. Add salt, pepper and stock. Cook for 30 minutes.

Add fruit. Continue to simmer until chicken is done.

Serve over white rice.

Chicken and Green Chile Enchiladas

Serves 5

1	small onion, chopped
1	carrot, sliced
4	cups hot water
2	whole chicken breasts
	salt to taste
4	long green chilies, roasted, peeled and deveined
3	tablespoons butter
3	tablespoons flour
1	cup milk
1	ripe avocado
1	medium onion, finely chopped
¾	pound Monterey Jack cheese, grated
10	corn tortillas, fresh, if possible
	oil
1	cup sour cream

Cook onion and carrot in water until tender. Add chicken breasts. Poach until tender, about 10 minutes. Do not overcook. Remove chicken from broth when cooled. Reserve broth. Skin, dice and salt chicken lightly.

Blend broth, carrots, onions and chilies in blender.

Combine butter and flour in saucepan. Cook slightly. Add 3 cups of blended broth, leaving 1 cup in blender. Add milk. Cook and stir until thickened.

Add pulp of avocado to broth in blender. Blend until smooth. Add avocado mixture to sauce in pan and stir until mixed. Keep sauce warm.

Cook each tortilla separately in hot oil until soft. Fill each tortilla with chicken, onion and cheese. Roll up each tortilla and place in greased flat casserole, seam side down. Cover with sauce. Top with remaining grated cheese and sour cream. Keep hot until ready to serve.

When handling chilies, wear rubber gloves to prevent oils from coming in contact with your skin.

Cafe Chili Blanco

Serves 8

This recipe can be easily doubled and doubled again!

1	pound dried great Northern white beans, rinsed well and picked over
2	pounds bone–in chicken breasts, cooked as directed below
1	tablespoon olive oil
2	medium onions, chopped
4	garlic cloves, chopped
2	4–ounce cans chopped mild green chilies
2	teaspoons ground cumin
1½	teaspoons dried oregano, crumbled
¼	teaspoon ground cloves
¼	teaspoon cayenne pepper
6	cups chicken stock or canned chicken broth
	salt and pepper to taste

Garnish:

3	cups Monterey Jack cheese, grated
	sour cream
	salsa
	fresh cilantro, chopped

Place beans in large pot. Add cold water to cover by 3 inches. Soak overnight. Drain when ready to use.

Place chicken breasts into large saucepan. Add cold water, onion, celery, carrot, salt and pepper. Bring to simmer. Cook just until tender, about 15 minutes. Drain and cool. Remove skin and bones. Cut chicken into cubes.

In same pan, sauté onions in oil until translucent, about 10 minutes. Stir in garlic, chilies, cumin, oregano, cloves and cayenne. Sauté 2 minutes. Add beans and stock. Bring to boil. Reduce to simmer until beans are very tender, about 2 hours. Stir occasionally.

Add chicken and 1 cup cheese to chili. Stir until cheese melts. Season to taste with salt and pepper. Ladle chili into bowls.

Serve with remaining cheese, sour cream, salsa and cilantro.

Soup may be prepared in advance. Cover and refrigerate before adding chicken and 1 cup cheese. Bring to a simmer after removing from refrigerator and proceed with preparation.

☙ *I wish I had time to have just one more bowl of chili.*

—dying words of Kit Carson

Glazed Cornish Game Hens

Serves 4

2	24-ounce Cornish game hens
2	teaspoons butter, softened
	salt and pepper to taste
½	cup toasted bread crumbs
	or
	crushed croutons
½	cup mushrooms, coarsely chopped
½	cup onions, finely chopped
2	tablespoons soy sauce
¼	cup butter, melted
¼	cup olive oil
¼	teaspoon rosemary leaves, crushed
1	tablespoon honey
1	teaspoon Dijon mustard

Preheat oven to 350°.

Rinse hens inside and out. Pat dry. Rub cavities with butter and season with salt and pepper.

Combine bread crumbs, mushrooms and onions. Fill cavities with stuffing. Truss. Place hens in shallow roasting pan. Bake 45 minutes.

Combine soy sauce, butter, oil, rosemary, honey and mustard. Pour sauce over hens and bake additional 30 minutes, basting occasionally.

Anna's Chicken Curry

Serves 6 to 8

3	cups onion, chopped
3	tablespoons fresh ginger, minced
4	garlic cloves, minced
¼	cup canola oil
2	pounds boneless chicken, cubed
2–3	tablespoons curry powder
¾	cup chicken broth, defatted
1	tablespoon dry sherry
1	teaspoon cornstarch
3	cups cooked rice, warmed

Sauté onion, ginger and garlic in oil in Dutch oven. Add chicken and cook until brown. Stir in curry powder. Add broth and bring to boil. Cover, reduce heat and simmer 25 minutes. Remove chicken from pan. Keep warm.

Combine sherry and cornstarch in small bowl. Add to liquid in Dutch oven. Bring to boil and cook 1 minute. Return chicken to pan. Heat thoroughly. Serve over rice with chutney and your favorite condiments.

Pheasant with Marrons Glacés

Serves 6 to 8

May be prepared and frozen.

2	whole pheasants
3–4	tablespoons olive oil
½	pound pearl onions, peeled
1–2	tablespoons flour
	grated rind and juice of 2 oranges
2	tablespoons red burgundy wine
2	cups rich stock
2	tablespoons red currant jelly
1	bouquet garni
2	cans marrons glacés
	salt and pepper
½	cup parsley, chopped

Using ovenproof pan, brown pheasant on all sides in olive oil. Remove pheasant. Sauté onions in same pan until golden brown. Remove from pan. Stir flour into remaining oil.

Add all ingredients in order, omitting marrons glacés, salt, pepper and parsley. Bring to boil, stirring often. Season with salt and pepper to taste. Return pheasant to pan. Add onions and marrons glacés. Cover and bake for 1½ to 2 hours at 325°.

Remove pheasant, onions and marrons from pan. Reduce sauce and thicken slightly with flour, if necessary. Carefully take meat from bones and put aside.

Pour half of sauce into casserole. Add pheasant, onions and marrons. Cover with remaining sauce. Garnish with chopped parsley and serve.

Chicken Fonda

Serves 4

This recipe was supposedly one of Henry Fonda's favorites.

3	tablespoons milk
3	tablespoons butter or margarine, melted
¼	cup Dijon mustard
½	cup honey
1	teaspoon curry powder or to taste
1	teaspoon salt
4	chicken breasts, boned
	brown rice or couscous

Preheat oven to 350°.

Mix milk, melted butter, mustard, honey, curry powder and salt in bowl until thoroughly blended. Roll chicken breasts in mixture, coating each piece well.

Place chicken breasts in roasting pan. Bake at 350° for 1 hour or until chicken is golden brown. Baste chicken about every 15 minutes with curry mixture.

Serve with brown rice or couscous and pass additional sauce.

Vegetables

Colorful vegetables served with just meat or fish can elevate ordinary fare into a feast.

—P.K. Smith

Green Beans and Tomatoes with Basil

Serves 4 to 6

For a different taste treat, substitute other fresh vegetables for green beans.

1	pound green beans, washed and trimmed
1	garlic clove, pressed
3	tablespoons unsalted butter
5	tablespoons fresh basil leaves, minced
	or
5	teaspoons dried basil, crumbled
5	small tomatoes, quartered
	salt and pepper to taste

Cook green beans in boiling, salted water for 4 to 5 minutes. Refresh beans immediately in cold water.

Sauté garlic in melted butter over moderately low heat for 2 minutes. Add green beans and ⅔ of basil. Stir the mixture until beans are heated through. Add tomatoes, remaining basil, salt and pepper. Heat mixture, tossing gently, until tomatoes are heated through.

Baked Asparagus

Serves 2 to 3

1	bunch asparagus
2	tablespoons olive oil
3	tablespoons sesame seeds
4	tablespoons Parmesan cheese, grated

Preheat oven to 400°.

Wash asparagus and trim ends. Place on jelly roll pan. Drizzle with olive oil. Sprinkle with sesame seeds and Parmesan cheese.

Bake for 12 to 15 minutes or until asparagus is tender. Place under broiler for 2 minutes to brown sesame seeds and melt cheese.

 Asparagus is a perennial plant of the lily family native to Western Asia. Highly prized for its succulent young stems, it is often grown in flower gardens for its delicate, ornamental foliage.

Cordon Bleu Tomatoes Provençal

3	tomatoes
2	shallots, minced
4	green onions, sliced
1	garlic clove, minced
2	tablespoons parsley, minced
7	tablespoons olive oil, divided

Preheat oven to 375°.

Cut tomatoes in half. Sprinkle with salt. Sauté shallots, green onions, garlic and parsley in 3 tablespoons olive oil.

Heat 4 tablespoons oil in ovenproof skillet. Add tomatoes, cut surface down, and fry for 3 minutes. Turn tomatoes and cover each surface with onion and garlic mixture. Bake for 5 minutes.

Baked Tomatoes

3	large tomatoes
	salt and pepper to taste
2	tablespoons Dijon mustard
½	cup light sour cream
3	scallions, including some green, sliced
¼	teaspoon garlic powder
	fresh parsley, chopped

Preheat oven to 500°.

Cut tomatoes in half. Place on baking sheet. Sprinkle with salt and pepper.

Combine remaining ingredients. Spread on tomatoes. Bake for 6 to 8 minutes or until heated through. Garnish with parsley.

❸ *The word "tomato" from the ancient Aztec "tomatl".*
Tomatoes were first grown in America by Thomas Jefferson
in his Monticello gardens.

Baked Fennel

Serve 8

This would also be a superb first course!

4	fennel bulbs
1	quart beef stock
¾	cup white wine
	salt and pepper to taste
8	teaspoons butter
½	cup Gruyère cheese, grated
⅓	cup Fontina cheese, grated
⅓	cup Parmesan cheese, grated

Preheat oven to 350°.

Trim stalk from bulbs. Cut each bulb in half lengthwise. Place in large saucepan. Pour stock and wine over bulbs. Simmer 10 to 15 minutes until tender. Drain.

Place fennel cut side down in one layer in large, buttered ovenproof dish. Add salt and pepper. Put 1 teaspoon butter on each bulb and sprinkle with cheeses. Bake for 10 to 12 minutes until cheese bubbles.

❧ *The ancient Greeks and Romans grew fennel for its delicious stalks as well as its dried seeds, which have a licorice flavor. During the Middle Ages, fennel was believed to prevent witchcraft, improve eyesight and give courage.*

Creamed Cabbage

Serves 6

This is a new way to fix an old standby.

3	tablespoons butter
1	garlic clove, minced
8	cups cabbage, shredded
¼	cup Chablis wine
1	egg, slightly beaten
⅓	cup sour cream
1	tablespoon lemon juice
1	tablespoon sugar
1	teaspoon salt
½	teaspoon celery seed

Melt butter in large skillet. Add garlic and cook over low heat. Add cabbage and wine. Simmer for 15 minutes until cabbage is tender, stirring occasionally.

Combine remaining ingredients with cabbage and serve.

Red Cabbage, Danish Style

erves 6

*ou can prepare this
day ahead.*

1	medium head red cabbage, about 2 ½ pounds
4	tablespoons butter, cut into small pieces
1	tablespoon brown sugar
1	teaspoon sugar
1	teaspoon salt
⅓	cup water
⅓	cup white vinegar
¼	cup red currant jelly
2	tablespoons apple, grated

Preheat oven to 325°.

Wash cabbage and remove tough outer leaves. Cut head in half, top to bottom. Lay flat side down on chopping board. Cut away core and slice cabbage very thin. Yield should be approximately 9 cups.

Combine butter, sugars, salt, water and vinegar in a 5–quart heavy enamel casserole. Heat until butter is melted. Add cabbage. Toss with fork when boiling starts again.

Cover tightly and place in center of oven to braise for 2 hours. Add water, if necessary. Add jelly and apple 10 minutes before cabbage is finished. Cover to complete cooking.

Let rest one day in refrigerator. Reheat in oven at 325° for 25 minutes.

Caramelized Onions

erves 4

ood with pork, beef or lamb.

3	pounds large sweet yellow onions
	salt and pepper to taste
2	cups chicken stock
2	teaspoons sherry wine vinegar
1	tablespoon balsamic vinegar
1	cup half and half

Slice onions into thin rounds. Season generously with salt and pepper. Put onions, stock and vinegars in large saucepan. Stir frequently until stock evaporates and onions caramelize, about 25 to 30 minutes. Simmer onions gently.

Add cream to onions, gradually. Keep warm until ready to serve.

Sugar Snap Pea Stir-Fry

Serves 4 to 6

¾	pound sugar snap peas
½	tablespoon peanut oil
1	teaspoon fresh ginger, minced
½	tablespoon oriental sesame oil
	pinch sugar
	pinch salt

Pull off stems of peas.

Heat oil in wok or heavy skillet. Add ginger and stir–fry for several seconds. Add peas and stir–fry until they turn very bright green.

Season with sesame oil, sugar and salt. Serve hot or at room temperature.

Brussels Sprouts with Water Chestnuts

Serves 6

2	10–ounce packages frozen Brussels sprouts, steamed slightly
1	can water chestnuts
1	teaspoon sugar
1½	teaspoons seasoned salt
¼	cup parsley, chopped
¼	cup butter

Halve large sprouts.

Drain water chestnuts, reserving juice, and chop.

Add water to chestnut juice to equal 1 cup. Combine liquid with sugar, seasoned salt and parsley in small sauce pan. Bring to boil.

Add Brussels sprouts. Cover and simmer until tender-crisp, about 10 minutes. Drain liquid Add butter and chestnuts.

 ☻ *A water chestnut is the edible tuber of a water plant
indigenous to Southeast Asia. Its flesh is white, crunchy
and juicy. It can also be dried, ground into flour and used
as a thickener in Oriental cooking.*

Brussels Sprouts Gratin

Serves 6

Easy and elegant dish for entertaining!

2	pounds Brussels sprouts
8	strips lean bacon
	salt and pepper
¼	cup cream
⅓	cup bread crumbs

Preheat oven to 350°.

Parboil Brussels sprouts for 12 minutes. Drain and chop coarsely

Cook bacon gently until crisp. Remove and drain bacon, reserving 4 tablespoons bacon drippings.

Add chopped Brussels sprouts to drippings in skillet. Stir over high heat. Add salt and pepper to taste. Stir in crumbled bacon. Pour into a buttered 9 x 13–inch au gratin dish. Pour cream over the top and sprinkle with bread crumbs.

Bake for 25 minutes.

Braised Spinach and Shallots

Serves 6

2	tablespoons butter
2	tablespoons extra virgin olive oil
4-5	shallots, minced
3	10–ounce packages frozen chopped spinach, thawed and drained
1	teaspoon salt
	fresh nutmeg, grated
	additional butter to finish dish

Sauté shallots in butter and oil until tender, but not brown. Add spinach. Season with salt and generous amount of nutmeg.

Toss spinach over high heat until liquid is evaporated. Remove from heat.

Finish by stirring in about 1 tablespoon butter.

The neglected shallot is the link between the onion and the garlic. Like garlic, it is divided into cloves. Unlike garlic, it does not linger on the breath.

Purée of Potatoes and Rutabaga with Bacon

Serves 8

Reheats in microwave beautifully!

6	russet potatoes
2	sweet potatoes or yams
1	cup milk, heated
4	tablespoons butter, divided
1	small rutabaga, peeled and cubed
6	bacon slices, diced and sautéed
2	tablespoons parsley, finely chopped
	salt and pepper

Preheat oven to 400°.

Wash and prick potatoes. Bake until done. Remove from skins. Immediately put through ricer or food mill. Add warm milk until desired consistency is attained. Add 3 tablespoons butter.

Simmer rutabaga in water to cover until tender. Put through food mill directly into potatoes or use food processor. Season with salt and pepper. Stir in bacon and parsley. Drizzle with remaining butter.

Sweet Potato Casserole

Serves 6

6	medium sweet potatoes, unpeeled
4-6	tablespoons butter or margarine
¼	teaspoon cinnamon
¼	teaspoon mace
⅓	cup cream
⅓	cup cognac
	salt and pepper to taste
	almonds, chopped

Preheat oven to 375°.

Boil potatoes, covered, until tender. Drain, cool, peel and whip potatoes. Mix in butter, cinnamon, mace, cream, cognac, salt and pepper.

Place in ungreased casserole. Dot with butter. Sprinkle with almonds.

Bake 30 minutes.

Potatoes Italian

4	large baking potatoes
1	tablespoon olive oil
3	medium tomatoes, sliced
1	large Spanish onion, peeled and sliced thick
¼	cup Parmesan cheese, grated
½	cup mozzarella cheese, shredded
½	teaspoon oregano
1½	teaspoons salt
⅛	teaspoon pepper
2	tablespoons butter

Preheat oven to 400°.

Peel and slice potatoes ¼ inch thick. Arrange the potatoes, tomatoes and onion slices in layers in oiled 9 x 13–inch casserole. Sprinkle each layer with cheeses and seasonings. Dot with butter.

Bake, uncovered, for 50 minutes or until vegetables are tender and the top is crusty brown.

Rutabaga Turnip Purée

1½	pounds rutabaga, peeled and cup up
1	pound turnips, peeled and cut up
4	cups beef or chicken broth
4	tablespoons butter
¼	cup heavy cream
	salt and ground pepper to taste

Cook turnips and rutabagas in broth until tender and soft. Drain.

Place in food processor with butter, cream, salt and pepper to taste. Purée until smooth.

Place in microwave container and heat before serving.

Mushroom Pie

Serves 6

1	pie shell, baked
5	tablespoons unsalted butter
2	cups yellow onions, sliced
½	pound button mushrooms, sliced
½	pound oyster mushrooms, sliced
1	tablespoon Cognac
1	tablespoon flour
1	teaspoon lemon juice
¼	teaspoon pepper, freshly ground
½	teaspoon dill
½	cup heavy cream
1	egg

Preheat oven to 325°.

Sauté onions in butter until golden. Add mushrooms and continue to cook 2 to 3 minutes. Add Cognac, flour, lemon juice and spices to pan.

Mix cream and egg together and fold into onion and mushroom mixture. Continue to cook 1 minute. Allow mixture to cool.

Spoon cooled mixture into cooked pie shell. Bake for 40 to 45 minutes.

Cool and serve at room temperature.

Southern Corn Pudding

Serves 6 to 8

This is a recipe from a Kentucky grandmother, born in 1856. Delicious!

4-6	ears fresh corn
2	cups milk, scalded
3	eggs, slightly beaten
¼	teaspoon salt
3	tablespoons sugar
	sprinkle of black pepper

Preheat oven to 350°.

Split corn down each row and scrape off kernels with back of knife. Scald milk in double boiler.

Put all ingredients together in casserole. Dot with butter. Set casserole in pan of hot water. Bake 1 hour and 45 minutes or until silver knife comes out clean.

If a flat glass pan is used, set in hot water and bake only 60 minutes.

This will keep three days in the refrigerator, if there is any left!

Mexican Spoon Bread

Serves 8

A wonderful substitute for potatoes with any kind of meat or poultry.

1	cup yellow cornmeal
1	teaspoon salt
½	teaspoon baking soda
¾	cup milk
⅓	cup vegetable oil
2	eggs, beaten
1	17–ounce can cream style corn
1	4–ounce can mild green chilies, chopped
1½	cups Monterey Jack cheese, grated

Mix cornmeal, salt and soda. Stir in milk and oil. Mix well. Add eggs and corn. Mix well.

Spoon half of the mixture into a greased 9 x 9 baking pan. Sprinkle ½ of chilies on top, then ½ of cheese. Repeat layers, ending with cheese.

Bake at 350° for 45 minutes or until wooden pick inserted into the center comes out clean. Spoon from the pan to serve.

Spanish Onion Pie

Serves 6

¼	cup unsalted butter, melted
1	cup Ritz crackers, crumbled
2	cups Spanish onions, thinly sliced
2	tablespoons butter
2	eggs
¾	cup milk
¾	teaspoon salt
	aged Swiss, Baby Swiss or Jarlsberg cheese, grated

Preheat oven to 350° for 30 minutes.

Combine melted butter and cracker crumbs. Press into 9–inch pie plate to form crust.

Sauté onions in butter until softened. Drain and place in pie shell.

Beat eggs, milk and salt together. Pour carefully over onions in pie shell. Sprinkle generously with grated cheese in any combination.

Bake 30 minutes.

Tuscan–Style Sautéed White Beans

Serves 6

2	tablespoons olive oil
½	cup fresh sage, chopped
	or
½	cup fresh parsley, chopped, and 1 teaspoon dried sage
2	garlic cloves, pressed
4	cups cooked or canned cannellini beans, drained
	salt and pepper to taste
6	Roma tomatoes, peeled, seeded and chopped
1	cup chicken broth, if needed

Heat olive oil in broad skillet. Add sage or parsley and cook briefly. Add garlic and cook 1 minute. Add beans and combine well. Season with salt and pepper.

Add tomatoes. Continue cooking for 10 minutes.

Add chicken broth if beans become too dry during cooking.

Apple–Stuffed Squash

Serves 6

Delicious and a wonderful addition to pork.

3	small acorn squash, cut lengthwise and seeded
2	apples, peeled, cored and diced
½	cup cashews, coarsely chopped
¼	cup butter or margarine, melted
¼	cup maple syrup

Preheat oven to 400°.

In a large Dutch oven, place squash, cut side down, on a steamer rack over boiling water. Steam about 20 minutes. Transfer squash, upright, to two 9–inch square baking dishes. Set aside.

Mix remaining ingredients together. Spoon into squash cavities. Pour hot water ½ inch deep into the dishes.

Cover and bake for 25 minutes.

☉ *Salt added to apples improves flavor and makes them more tender.*

Vegetable Array

Serves 6

½	cup olive oil
2	garlic cloves
2	teaspoons fresh thyme
2	teaspoons fresh sage, chopped
	salt and pepper to taste
3	red bell peppers, seeded and cut into strips
3	green peppers, seeded and quartered
2	small Japanese eggplants, halved
2	small yellow squash, crookneck or pattypan
2	zucchini, halved and quartered
1	large red onion, thick slices

Combine oil, garlic and herbs. Let stand 1 hour.

Brush vegetables with oil mixture. Salt and pepper to taste. Grill until tender, about 8 minutes, turning and watching closely.

Cold Broccoli with Cashews

Serves 8

A wonderful choice for a summer menu or picnic!

3	pounds broccoli
½	cup olive oil
¼	cup fresh lemon juice
½	teaspoon salt
	pepper to taste
4	teaspoons fresh chervil
½	cup salted cashews, coarsely broken

Cook broccoli until just tender. Place in serving dish.

Combine oil, lemon juice, salt, pepper and chervil. Pour over broccoli, cover and chill.

Sprinkle with cashews just before serving.

This should be prepared at least 8 hours in advance.

To vary, experiment with fresh asparagus or fresh green beans and any herb snipped from your garden.

Party Potatoes

2	pounds potatoes, cooked, peeled and sliced
5	tablespoons butter
5	tablespoons flour
2	cups half and half, scalded
⅔	cup chicken stock
5	teaspoons Parmesan cheese, freshly grated
1	teaspoon salt
½	teaspoon white pepper, freshly ground
¾	cup Roquefort cheese, crumbled
¼	cup butter, melted
	paprika

Overlap potato slices in 2–quart au gratin dish.

Melt 5 tablespoons butter in saucepan. Add flour and whisk over low heat for 2 minutes. Remove pan from heat and gradually stir in cream and stock. Return pan to heat and stir sauce until it is smooth and thickened. Stir in Parmesan. Add salt and pepper to taste.

Pour sauce over arranged potatoes. Sprinkle with Roquefort cheese, melted butter and paprika.

Bake at 425° for 20 to 25 minutes or until cheese bubbles.

Eggplant Parmigiana

1	medium eggplant, peeled and sliced ¼ inch thick
1	egg
2	tablespoons milk
2	tablespoons flour
¼	teaspoon salt
1	16–ounce can tomato sauce
½	cup Parmesan cheese, freshly grated
4	ounces Mozzarella cheese, sliced
	vegetable oil

Beat together egg, milk, flour and salt to make a batter. Dip eggplant slices in batter and fry in vegetable oil until brown.

Alternate layers of eggplant slices, sauce and cheeses in greased 1½–quart casserole, ending with cheeses.

Bake at 350° for 30 minutes.

Beets with Horseradish

Serves 4

Great for beet lovers and it can be done in the microwave!

Horseradish Sauce:

3	tablespoons fresh horseradish, grated
2	tablespoons mayonnaise
2	tablespoons sour cream
½	teaspoon Dijon mustard
½	teaspoon white wine vinegar

Beets:

8	medium beets, washed and trimmed of all but 2 inches of stem
¾	cup water
1	tablespoon unsalted butter
1	tablespoon prepared horseradish sauce
3	tablespoons half and half
	salt and pepper to taste
	parsley or dill for garnish

Combine horseradish, mayonnaise, sour cream, mustard and vinegar to make sauce.

Place beets in 2–quart microwave casserole. Add water and cover. Cook on high for 18 to 22 minutes, turning dish once every 6 minutes, until tender. Uncover, cool, remove skins, trim ends and slice into ¼ inch slices.

Wipe out casserole, add butter and melt on high for 30 seconds. Stir in the horseradish sauce, half and half, salt and pepper. Add beets, turning to coat with mixture. Cover and cook on high for 1½ minutes or until heated through.

Garnish with parsley or dill and serve.

Oven–Fried Eggplant

Serves 4 to 6

1	pound eggplant, sliced ½ inch thick
½	cup fine dry bread or cracker crumbs
¼	cup Parmesan cheese, grated
¼	cup mayonnaise

Preheat oven to 425°.

Mix crumbs and cheese. Spread mayonnaise on both sides of eggplant slices and coat with crumb mixture.

Bake 15 minutes or until browned.

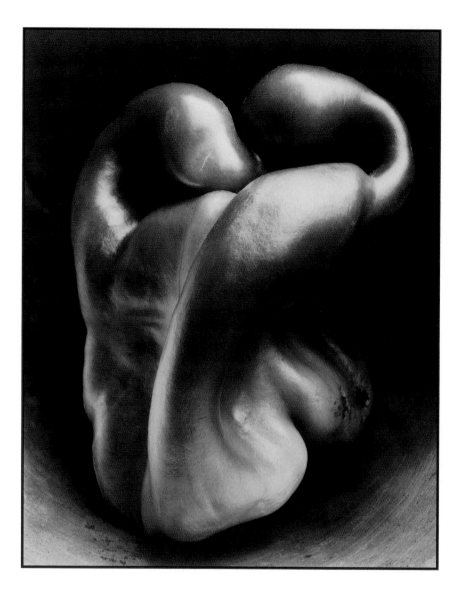

EDWARD WESTON
Pepper No. 30, 1930
Bequest of Dorothy Millett Lindeke

Metate in the Form of a Jaguar, Costa Rican, 10th–13th century
The Ethel Morrison Van Derlip Fund

Esther and Ahasuerus, Flemish, 1475–85
Gift of Mrs. C. J. Martin for the Charles Jairus Martin Memorial Collection

Desserts

What would you like for dessert?
Anything, as long as it is chocolate.

—*Anonymous*

Triple Chocolate Cookies

Yields 8 dozen

5¼	cups chocolate chips, divided
6	ounces baking chocolate
¾	cup margarine
6	eggs
1½	cups granulated sugar
1	tablespoon plus ½ teaspoon instant coffee
6	tablespoons flour
½	teaspoon baking powder
½	teaspoon salt
2¼	cups pecans, chopped
2¼	cups walnuts, chopped

Melt 2¼ cups chocolate chips, baking chocolate and margarine together. Beat eggs, sugar and coffee together until fluffy. Add to chocolate mixture.

Combine flour, baking powder and salt. Add to chocolate mixture. Mix until just blended.

Stir remaining chocolate chips and nuts into batter. Drop rounded tablespoons onto parchment–lined baking sheets.

Bake at 350° for 10 to 12 minutes. Center should remain soft and fudge–like.

Almond Cookies

Yield about 50

Sprinkle with colored sugars for the holidays!

½	pound butter or half butter and half margarine
½	cup granulated sugar
2	cups flour
½–1	teaspoon almond extract
1	cup almonds, finely chopped or ground
	sugar

Preheat oven to 325°.

Cream butter and sugar. Add flour and extract. Blend well. Add ground nuts. Form into 2 long rolls about ½ inch in diameter. Wrap in plastic and refrigerate for at least 8 hours.

Remove from refrigerator 10 minutes before slicing. Slice into rounds ¼ inch thick.

Bake on greased or non–stick cookie sheet for about 10 minutes or until lightly browned. Sprinkle with sugar immediately.

Ginger Pecan Cookies

Yield 3 dozen

Thin and crisp.

1	cup flour
½	teaspoon baking soda
¼	teaspoon ginger
¼	teaspoon ground cloves
¼	teaspoon ground cinnamon
¼	teaspoon ground nutmeg
6	ounces unsalted butter
¼	cup granulated sugar
½	cup dark brown sugar
1	egg, slightly beaten
½	cup pecans, chopped
½	cup crystallized ginger, chopped

Preheat oven to 350°.

Combine flour, baking soda and spices in bowl. Stir with whisk.

Beat butter and sugars in separate bowl at medium speed 4 to 5 minutes until light and fluffy. Add beaten egg a little at a time and beat another 3 to 4 minutes. Gradually fold in flour mixture by hand. Add pecans and ginger.

Drop dough by teaspoons on well–buttered cookie sheet 1½ inches apart.

Bake at 350° for 13 to 15 minutes until golden brown. Cool on wire rack.

Chocolate Thins

Yield 2 dozen

1	cup sugar
3	tablespoons butter, melted
2	eggs, beaten
2	squares chocolate
	pinch of salt
3½	tablespoons flour
1	teaspoon vanilla
½–¾	cup pecans, broken

Combine first 4 ingredients. Stir in flour, vanilla and nuts. Drop by teaspoons on greased or non–stick cookie sheet 2 to 3 inches apart.

Bake in 350° oven for 3 to 4 minutes or until they stop bubbling. Cool for a moment and remove.

Favorite Ginger Snaps

¾	cup butter and shortening combined
1	cup granulated sugar
1	egg
4	tablespoons molasses
2	cups flour, sifted
1	teaspoon baking soda
1	teaspoon ground cloves
1	teaspoon ginger
1	teaspoon cinnamon
	granulated sugar for dipping

Preheat oven to 350°.

Cream together butter, shortening and sugar. Add egg and molasses. Blend well. Add flour, baking soda and spices. Beat until well combined.

Roll small amounts of dough in palm of hand to size of large marbles. Dip in dish of granulated sugar. Place on greased cookie sheet not close together, as they flatten out while baking.

Bake for 10 to 12 minutes or to a light color.

Ginger Lace Cookies

1	cup sugar
¼	cup margarine
⅓	cup dark molasses
1	egg
2	cups flour
2	teaspoons baking powder
1	teaspoon ginger
1	teaspoon cinnamon
½	teaspoon salt
	sugar for dipping

Combine dry ingredients and set aside. Combine sugar, margarine, molasses and egg, blending well. Combine dry ingredients with molasses mixture. Stir well. Add water, 1 teaspoon at a time, if dough appears too thick.

Roll dough into 1–inch balls and dip in granulated sugar. Place on lightly greased cookie sheet, allowing for spreading.

Bake at 350° for 8 to 10 minutes.

Orange Drop Cookies

Chocolate lovers may add a chocolate glaze!

⅓	cup butter
⅓	cup shortening
¾	cup sugar
1	egg
½	cup orange juice
2	tablespoons orange rind, grated
2	cups flour
½	teaspoon baking powder
½	teaspoon baking soda
½	teaspoon salt

Frosting:

2½	tablespoons soft butter
1½	cups powdered sugar, unsifted
1½	tablespoons orange juice
2	tablespoons orange rind, grated

Cream together butter, shortening and sugar. Beat in egg. Stir in orange juice and rind.

Sift together flour, baking powder, baking soda and salt. Blend with orange–butter mixture. Drop by teaspoons on ungreased cookie sheet.

Bake at 350° for approximately 8 minutes.

Blend butter and sugar for the icing. Add juice and rind. Mix until smooth and frost the cookies.

Crackerjack Cookies

Yield 4 dozen

Good and crunchy!

1	cup butter or margarine
¾	cup white sugar
¾	cup brown sugar, lightly packed
2	teaspoons vanilla
1	teaspoon soda
2	cups quick oatmeal
2	eggs
1½	cups flour, unsifted
1	teaspoon baking powder
2	cups Rice Krispies
½	cup nuts, chopped
1	small package butterscotch bits
1	cup coconut

Mix together and drop by teaspoons onto greased cookie sheet.

Bake at 350° for 10 minutes.

193

Pumpkin Raisin Oatmeal Cookies

1	cup flour
1	cup butter
1	cup brown sugar
½	cup sugar
1	cup canned pumpkin
½	teaspoon salt
½	teaspoon baking soda
1	egg
3	cups rolled oats
1	cup raisins

Preheat oven to 375°.

Combine first 8 ingredients. Add oats and raisins. Drop by rounded teaspoons onto greased cookie sheet.

Bake about 12 minutes.

Cranapple Crisp

Serves 6

4	cups tart apples, peeled and sliced
⅓–½	cup dried cranberries
¼	cup pecans, chopped
⅔–¾	cup brown sugar
½	cup all–purpose flour
½	cup oatmeal
¾	teaspoon cinnamon
¾	teaspoon nutmeg
⅓	cup margarine, softened

Toppings:

½	cup heavy cream, whipped and sweetened, crème fraîche, frozen vanilla yogurt or French vanilla ice cream, softened

Heat oven to 375°. Grease square 8 x 8 x 2–inch pan. Place apple slices in pan. Sprinkle with cranberries and nuts.

Mix remaining ingredients and sprinkle over apples.

Bake 30 minutes or until apples are tender and topping is brown. Top with one of the optional toppings.

Biscuit Tortoni

½	cup red and green candied cherries, chopped
2	tablespoons Marsala wine
1	cup whipping cream
6	tablespoons confectioners' sugar, divided
2	egg whites
	pinch cream of tartar
½	cup Almond Macaroon* crumbs
12	foil baking cup liners
¼	cup slivered almonds, toasted

Marinate cherries in Marsala wine while preparing remaining ingredients.

Beat whipping cream with 3 tablespoons confectioners' sugar until thick and firm.

Add cream of tartar to egg whites. Beat until frothy. Add remaining confectioners' sugar gradually to egg whites. Continue to beat until firm peaks form.

Fold together whipped cream, beaten egg whites, cherries and Almond Macaroon* crumbs. Spoon mixture into foil baking cup liners. Garnish tops with almonds.

Place in freezer. After tortoni are frozen, cover with plastic wrap to prevent freezer burn.

Place frozen tortoni, in baking cups, on doily–covered individual serving plates. Arrange almond macaroon beside tortoni.

Almond Macaroons

Yields 24

8	ounces almond paste
1	cup granulated sugar
2	egg whites

Place almond paste in bowl of food processor. Process until smooth.

Add sugar and egg whites. Process until fluffy.

Make 1 inch mounds of mixture, using two teaspoons. Place on oiled baking sheet. Flatten mounds slightly with back of spoon.

Bake at 325° for 25 minutes, or until slightly browned. Remove from cookie sheet while still warm.

Autumn Apple Cake with Sauce

Cake:

2	cups sugar
½	cup butter
2	eggs, beaten
2¼	cups flour, sifted
2	teaspoons baking soda
2	teaspoons cinnamon
1	teaspoon nutmeg
	pinch of salt
4	cups apples, diced
1	cup nuts, optional

Sauce:

½	cup melted butter
1	cup brown sugar
1	cup sugar
1	cup cream
2	teaspoons vanilla

Cream together sugar and butter. Add dry ingredients. Add apples and nuts. Batter will be very thick. Pour into greased 9 x 13–inch pan.

Bake at 350° for 45 minutes.

Cook sauce until thick and serve warm over cake.

Date–Pecan Chews

8	ounces dates, finely chopped
¼	pound butter
1	cup brown sugar
2	cups Rice Krispies
1	cup pecans, chopped
1	cup flaked coconut
1	teaspoon vanilla
1	teaspoon fennel seed, crushed

Cook butter, brown sugar and dates slowly in heavy pan until mixture bubbles. Use wooden spoon to stir. Add remaining ingredients, mixing well.

Press flat in buttered 8 x 12– inch pan. Cut into strips when cool and roll in powdered sugar.

☻ *Store any unused pecans in the freezer to preserve their sweet, southern flavor.*

Chocolate Banana Cake

½	cup butter
1¼	cups sugar
2	eggs
1	teaspoon baking soda
2	bananas
1	teaspoon vanilla
2	cups all–purpose flour
1	teaspoon baking powder
4	teaspoons cocoa, rounded
1	cup sour cream

Cream butter and sugar. Add eggs one at a time, beating well after each.

Sift dry ingredients and add alternately with sour cream, beginning and ending with dry ingredients.

Combine bananas and baking soda. Add banana mixture to batter. Mix well.

Butter and flour 9 x 13– inch pan. Use parchment paper to line pan for easier removal. Pour cake batter into pan.

Bake at 350° for 25 to 40 minutes. Reduce heat to 325° if using glass pan.

Chocolate keeps indefinitely in an airtight container.....locked!

Sue Zelickson

Arcola Quickie

1	pint vanilla ice cream
1½	cups pure maple syrup, Vermont if possible
½	cup walnuts, crushed

Heat maple syrup. Put ice cream in frappé glasses or other dishes. Pour one–quarter of the heated syrup over ice cream. Sprinkle with crushed walnuts.

For 4th of July, try vanilla ice cream with hot raspberry syrup and fresh blueberries.

Chocolate Angel Food Cake

Serves 16

Delicious and healthy. Serve with non–fat frozen yogurt and fresh raspberries.

¼	cup unsweetened cocoa powder, not Dutch
¼	cup coffee, hot and strong
1¼	cups sugar, divided
¾	cup cake flour, sifted
¼	teaspoon salt
12	egg whites
1	teaspoon cream of tartar

Preheat oven to 350°.

Dissolve cocoa in coffee in medium bowl. Cool to room temperature.

Combine ½ cup sugar, flour and salt.

Place egg whites in large mixing bowl and set over larger bowl of hot water. Stir for a few minutes until egg whites come to room temperature. Beat egg whites until frothy. Add cream of tartar and continue beating until soft peaks form. Gradually add remaining ¾ cup sugar and beat just until stiff peaks form. Do not over beat.

Sift flour mixture over beaten egg whites in three parts, folding in gently after each sifting. Stir 1 cup of egg white mixture into coffee mixture. Fold it back into egg white mixture until thoroughly combined.

Pour batter into ungreased 10–inch tube pan. Smooth top and run knife through batter to remove any air bubbles. Bake for 50 to 60 minutes or until cake tester comes out clean.

Invert pan over neck of bottle and cool completely. Loosen edges with knife and invert cake on serving platter.

θ *In 1890 Milton Hershey bought the first chocolate manufacturing machine and introduced the chocolate bar to the United States. Americans loved it! Every year each of us eats over eleven pounds of chocolate.*

Bitter Chocolate Cake

Serves 12 to 16

Rich, moist and gooey!

	sugar
1	cup unsalted butter
6	ounces semi–sweet chocolate, chopped
3	ounces unsweetened chocolate, chopped
1¼	cups sugar
4	eggs, extra large
1	tablespoon all–purpose flour
	whipping cream, whipped and lightly sweetened

Preheat oven to 325°.

Butter 9–inch springform pan. Sprinkle bottom and sides with sugar. Wrap foil around bottom and 2 inches up outside of pan.

Combine butter and both chocolates in top of double boiler. Melt over simmering water, stirring until smooth. Remove pan from water.

Whisk eggs and sugar in large bowl to blend. Mix in flour. Stir in warm chocolate mixture. Pour batter into prepared pan.

Place cake in large baking pan and pour enough boiling water into pan to reach at least half way up sides of springform pan.

Bake cake until top is firm and toothpick inserted into center comes out with some moist crumbs attached, about 1 hour.

Remove cake from water and remove foil. Cool completely on rack. Transfer cake to platter and release pan sides.

Cut into wedges and serve with whipped cream.

☻ *In ancient Mexico, the Aztec emperors permitted only the royal family to enjoy hot chocolate. Columbus brought cocoa beans back to Spain from the New World and the Spanish aristocracy enthusiastically relished the new treat.*

Tunnel of Fudge Cake

1	large size chocolate fudge or devils food cake mix, not super moist
1	3–ounce package instant chocolate fudge pudding mix
4	eggs
1	cup sour cream or sour half and half
½	cup vegetable oil
½	cup warm tap water
1	12–ounce package semisweet chocolate chips
	powdered sugar

Grease 12–cup bundt pan very well.

Combine cake mix, pudding mix, sour cream and eggs in mixing bowl. Beat 5 minutes.

Combine oil, water and chocolate chips. Mix briefly and quickly with fork and turn into cake batter. Pour into greased pan.

Bake about 50 minutes or until cake is pulling away from sides of pan. Cool 15 minutes in pan. Invert and cool on rack.

Sprinkle with powdered sugar. Serve with your favorite vanilla sauce, whipped cream or ice cream.

Tom Thumbs

Batter:

½	cup butter, softened
½	cup brown sugar, packed
½	teaspoon salt
1	cup sifted flour

Topping:

1	cup brown sugar
¼	teaspoon salt
1	teaspoon vanilla
2	eggs, well beaten
½	teaspoon baking powder
1	3½–ounce can flaked coconut
1	6–ounce package chocolate chips, optional

Combine batter ingredients. Spread in 7 x 11–inch pan.

Bake 15 minutes at 325°.

Combine topping ingredients and spread over warm crust layer.

Bake 25 additional minutes at 325° or until tests done.

Elegant Rum Cake

1	package yellow cake mix
½	cup rum

Filling:
2	cups heavy cream, whipped
¼	cup powdered sugar
1	teaspoon vanilla

Frosting:
6	squares unsweetened chocolate
1½	cups powdered sugar
3	tablespoons hot water
3	eggs
½	cup butter, softened
	nuts

Prepare and bake cake according to package directions. Cool. Cut each layer in half horizontally to make 4 layers. Sprinkle each layer with 2 tablespoons rum.

Whip cream and powdered sugar in small bowl. Add vanilla and beat until firm. Melt chocolate in double boiler. Beat in powdered sugar and hot water. Add eggs one at a time, beating well after each addition. Add butter and beat until smooth.

Place bottom layer on plate, cut side up. Spread with one–third of whipped cream filling. Repeat with next two layers. Top with last layer, cut side down.

Frost sides and top with chocolate frosting. Decorate with nuts around sides of cake.

Refrigerate overnight.

Danish Cream

Serves 6

1	envelope unflavored gelatin
¼	cup cold water
2½	cups heavy cream
1	cup sugar
2	cups sour cream
1	teaspoon vanilla

Dissolve gelatin in water. Heat cream, sugar and gelatin until dissolved. Cool.

Fold in sour cream and vanilla. Pour into mold and refrigerate until firm.

Serve with whole berries or puréed and sieved frozen raspberries.

Island Rum Cake

1	cup butter
1½	cups sugar
4	eggs
2	cups flour
2	teaspoons rum flavoring
2	teaspoons baking powder
2	cups pecans or walnuts, chopped
¾	cup sugar
½	cup water
½	cup light rum

Preheat oven to 325°.

Cream butter and sugar well with electric mixer in large bowl. Add eggs and mix until smooth. Add flour and rum flavoring. Add baking powder. Stir in nuts. Grease and flour tube pan. Pour mixture into pan and bake 1 hour on bottom rack of oven.

Combine sugar and water in medium sauce pan. Boil until sugar is dissolved. Remove from heat and add rum.

Pour warm rum sauce over cake while it is still warm. After sauce is absorbed, invert on serving plate.

Grilled Peaches with Blueberry Sauce

8	fresh peaches, quartered
¼	cup canola oil
Sauce:	
1	cup water
1	pint blueberries
1	cinnamon stick
½	cup sugar
1	bay leaf

Brush peaches with oil, grill lightly for about one minute.

Combine ingredients for sauce. Simmer for 10 minutes. Cool.

Serve warm peaches with lemon sherbet. Spoon blueberry sauce over both.

Try grilling pears or fresh pineapple to serve over orange–lemon–lime sherbet.

French Tart with Fresh Fruit

¼	cup lemon juice
1	teaspoon vanilla extract
½	cup sour cream
1	14–ounce can sweetened condensed milk
½	cup butter or margarine, softened
¼	cup brown sugar
1	cup flour
¼	cup rolled oats
¼	cup walnuts, chopped
	assorted fresh fruits: kiwi, strawberries, oranges, bananas, grapes

Preheat oven to 375°.

Combine lemon juice, vanilla, sour cream and condensed milk in medium bowl. Set aside to chill.

Beat butter and brown sugar until fluffy in large bowl. Add flour, oats and walnuts. Blend until creamy.

Press dough on cookie sheet to 12–inch circle or use tart pan. Rim edges of dough and prick base with fork.

Bake 10 to 12 minutes. Cool.

Spoon cooled filling onto crust. Arrange drained fruit on top of filling. Chill until serving time.

Pecan Pie, the Authentic One

A Southerner born and bred warns, "Don't fool around with other recipes. This is the only one!"

3	eggs
1	cup dark corn syrup
1	cup sugar
2	tablespoons butter, melted
1	teaspoon vanilla
⅛	teaspoon salt
1	cup pecans
1	9–inch pastry shell

Beat eggs slightly. Add next 5 ingredients. Stir in pecans. Pour into pastry shell.

Bake at 350° for 55 minutes or until knife inserted halfway between center and edge comes out clean. This test is important for success!

Pear Gorgonzola Tart

Crust:
4	ounces butter
1	egg
¾	cup sugar
	pinch of salt
1½	cups flour

Filling:
12	ounces cream cheese, room temperature
3	ounces Gorgonzola cheese
⅛	cup heavy cream
¼	cup sugar

Topping:
4	Bosc pears
4	cups port
2	cups sugar
½	cup water
1	small jar apricot preserves
	extra Gorgonzola, (optional)
	walnuts, chopped (optional)

Cream butter and sugar. Add egg and salt and combine. Add flour and mix until dough pulls together. Flatten ball and cover with plastic wrap. Refrigerate 1 hour.

Flour lightly and roll into 12–inch circle. Press into 10–inch tart shell pan. Remove excess dough from sides. Refrigerate until firm. Line tart with aluminum foil and fill with dried beans or pie weights. Bake at 350° for 15 minutes. Remove foil and bake until golden brown. Cool completely and remove from pan.

Mix cream cheese and sugar. Add heavy cream and Gorgonzola. Spread in bottom of baked tart shell.

Cut Bosc pears in half and remove core with melon baller. Slice unpeeled pears crosswise into thin sections. Heat port, sugar and water in medium pan, increasing water as needed to cover pears. Bring to boil. Add pear slices and simmer until just softened. Drain well and cool.

Arrange pear slices on tart filling in circular, overlapping pattern. Melt apricot preserves in small pan and brush lightly over pear slices. Sprinkle tart with extra Gorgonzola chunks and chopped walnuts, if desired.

Chill completely before slicing.

Nectarine Tart

Serves 8

Other fresh fruit in season could be used instead of nectarines.

⅓	cup butter
⅓	cup shortening
1½	teaspoons lemon peel, grated and divided
1½	cups sifted flour
⅓	cup powdered sugar
¼	teaspoon mace
1	8–ounce package cream cheese
2	tablespoons sugar
1	teaspoon vanilla
¼	cup whipping cream
4	cups nectarines, peeled and sliced
½	cup apricot jam
	mint sprigs for garnish

Preheat oven to 325°.

Cream together butter, shortening and 1 teaspoon lemon peel. Sift together flour, sugar, salt and mace. Stir into creamed mixture and form a ball. Pat into 11–inch tart pan.

Bake for 25 to 35 minutes or until crust is golden. Cool.

Soften cream cheese and beat until smooth. Beat in sugar, vanilla, ½ teaspoon lemon peel and cream. Spread over cooled crust. Arrange nectarines over cheese filling. Heat jam until thin and spread over fruit. Garnish with mint.

Old Fashioned Lemon Sponge Dessert

Serves 6 to 8

Could be served with a hot lemon sauce!

¾	cup sugar
¼	cup flour
2	teaspoons lemon rind, grated
⅓	cup lemon juice
3	egg yolks, beaten
3	egg whites, stiffly beaten
1½	cups milk, scalded and cooled
2	tablespoons butter, melted

Sift together sugar and flour. Combine dry ingredients, lemon rind and egg yolks. Beat well. Add milk and butter. Beat again. Add lemon juice. Beat well. Fold in egg whites.

Pour into greased ramekins and place in baking pan. Add water half way up sides of ramekins.

Bake at 375° for 45 minutes.

French Bread Pudding with Whiskey Sauce

Serves 6

An updated classic!

1	loaf French bread
1	quart milk
3	eggs, beaten
2	cups sugar
2	tablespoons vanilla
1	cup seedless raisins
¾	teaspoon ground cloves
½	teaspoon cinnamon
¼	teaspoon nutmeg
3	tablespoons butter or margarine, melted

Sauce:

1	stick butter
1	cup sugar
1	egg
	whiskey, bourbon, brandy or rum to taste

Break up bread and soak in milk, crushing with hands until well mixed. Add beaten eggs, 2 cups sugar, vanilla, raisins and spices. Stir well.

Pour melted butter into bottom of heavy 9 x 13–inch baking dish. Add bread mixture and bake at 300° until very firm, about 1 hour. Let cool.

Stirring constantly, bring butter, sugar and egg to boil over very low heat to make sauce. Continue stirring until slightly thickened. Add whiskey to taste.

Cube pudding and place in individual ovenproof dishes. Pour sauce over pudding when ready to serve. Heat under broiler.

Lemon Milk Sherbet

Serves 4–6

A light refreshing dessert. Serve with a fresh strawberry and a cookie on top!

1¼	cups granulated sugar
⅓	cup fresh lemon juice
	grated rind of one lemon
¼	teaspoon lemon extract
1	pint milk

Combine sugar, lemon juice, lemon extract and rind. Add milk. Stir until sugar dissolves.

Place in freezer until firm. Remove and beat with egg beater until fluffy.

Replace in freezer and cover.

Tiramisu

3	cups espresso coffee, cold
4	tablespoons Grand Marnier
30	ladyfingers
2	cups cream, whipped
6	egg yolks
6	tablespoons powdered sugar
2	tablespoons Marsala
1	pound mascarpone cheese
4	ounces dark chocolate, cubed

Pour coffee and Grand Marnier into shallow dish and dip 15 ladyfingers into mixture quickly. Line bottom of glass bowl with ladyfingers.

Whisk eggs and sugar together in large mixing bowl. Add mascarpone and Marsala and whisk until smooth. Fold mixture into whipped cream.

Spoon half of mascarpone mixture over ladyfingers and sprinkle half of chocolate over it. Layer remaining ladyfingers dipped in coffee mixture over top. Spoon remaining mascarpone mixture over this and top with remaining chocolate.

Cover and chill 6 hours before serving.

Chocolate Rum Mousse

¼	cup sugar
4	tablespoons white rum
4	ounces semi–sweet chocolate
3	tablespoons whipping cream
2	egg whites, stiffly beaten
1½	cups whipping cream, whipped
	shaved chocolate

Cook sugar and rum over very low heat until sugar is dissolved.

Melt chocolate in top of double boiler. Stir in 3 tablespoons of whipping cream when chocolate is melted.

Add rum mixture to chocolate mixture and stir until smooth. Cool, but do not chill. Fold in egg whites. Fold in whipped cream.

Pour into cups and chill at least 2 hours. Top with shaved chocolate and dot with whipped cream.

Fresh Peach Chantilly

Serves 8

An easy and perfect finale to any summer luncheon or dinner party.

3	egg whites
1	cup sugar
1	teaspoon baking powder
1	teaspoon vanilla
1	cup soda crackers, crushed
1	cup walnuts, chopped
1	cup whipping cream, whipped with 2 tablespoons powdered sugar
4	fresh peaches, peeled and sliced
	fresh mint or fresh sliced strawberries to garnish

Preheat oven to 350°.

Beat egg whites until stiff, but not dry. Add sugar gradually, beating until stiff peaks form. Add baking powder, vanilla, soda crackers and nuts. Pour into 9–inch greased pie plate. Bake for 35 minutes. Make crust day before serving.

Fill crust with whipped cream 4 hours before serving and refrigerate. Remove from refrigerator. Top with fresh peaches. Garnish with mint or berries before serving.

☻ *A little salt added to whipping cream or egg whites makes them whip up more rapidly with higher volume.*

Crêpes with Hot Lingonberries

Yield 16 crêpes

Great for brunch!

1	cup flour
1½	cups milk
3	eggs
	dash of salt
	lingonberry preserves
	vanilla ice cream

Combine flour, milk, eggs and salt in blender and beat at top speed for 30 seconds. Scrape down sides and blend for 15 seconds. Refrigerate for 2 hours. Cook the crêpes.

Heat lingonberry preserves.

To serve, scoop a little ice cream into crêpes. Top with hot lingonberry preserves.

Pumpkin Ice Cream Pie

24	2 x 2–inch graham crackers, crushed
½	cup butter or margarine, melted
½	cup sugar
1	15–ounce can pumpkin
1	cup brown sugar, packed
1	teaspoon salt
1	teaspoon ginger
1	teaspoon cinnamon
½	teaspoon nutmeg
2	quarts French vanilla ice cream
	whipped cream for garnish, optional

Preheat oven to 350°.

Combine crumbs, butter and sugar. Press into bottom of 9 x 13–inch pan.

Bake for 10 to 15 minutes. Cool.

Combine pumpkin, brown sugar, salt and spices. Beat for several minutes. Stir in softened ice cream. Pour into crust.

Freeze at least overnight or longer. Remove from freezer 15 minutes before serving. Top with whipped cream, if desired.

Pears in Champagne

4	ripe pears, halved, peeled and cored
1	cup water
1	cup sugar
1	quart lemon ice
	champagne

Make syrup of the sugar and water. Poach the pears in it 5 to 6 minutes.

Remove, drain and chill.

Make mound of the lemon ice. Lay the cold pear against it. Pour 3 ounces of champagne over each serving.

✆ *I am a teetotaler unless one is speaking of Champagne and then I always enjoy it.*

—*George Bernard Shaw*

Floating Island

4	egg whites
⅔	cup sugar
1	cup milk
1	cup light cream
4	egg yolks
½	cup sugar
1	vanilla bean, slit

Boil kettle of water. Beat egg whites until stiff, but not dry. Beat in sugar very gradually. Drop by tablespoons in boiling water, dipping spoon in cold water first. Poach each island for a few minutes, first on one side and then other. Place on paper towel to dry and cool.

Mix milk, cream and vanilla in top of double boiler. Beat egg yolks until thick and gradually add sugar. Add milk mixture a little at a time, beating after each addition. Return sauce to double boiler and cook until the custard coats spoon. Cool, stirring occasionally.

Pour custard onto individual dessert plates, top each with a floating island.

Buttermilk Pie

Makes two 9–inch pies

½	cup butter
4	cups sugar
8	tablespoons flour
1	teaspoon salt
4	eggs
2	cups buttermilk
2	tablespoons lemon juice
	nutmeg or vanilla, optional
2	9–inch pie shells, unbaked
	fresh fruit

Melt butter and blend with sugar, flour and salt. Add eggs, buttermilk, lemon juice and flavoring.

Bake in unbaked pie shells at 375° about 45 minutes or until pie does not shake.

Serve with sliced strawberries or other fresh fruit.

Caramelized Flan with Raspberries

Serves 8

Caramel:

3½	cups sugar, divided
½	cup water

Custard:

6	eggs
6	egg yolks
½	teaspoon nutmeg
2	tablespoons vanilla
2	cups heavy cream
2½	cups whole milk
2	pints raspberries
3	tablespoons Chambord

Preheat oven to 350°.

Mix 2 cups of sugar with water over low heat until sugar caramelizes. Pour mixture into one large flan pan or two small glass pie pans. Cover bottom and sides with caramelized mixture by rotating pan.

Mix eggs, yolks, nutmeg and vanilla in large bowl. Add cream and milk. Mix with 1½ cups sugar until sugar is dissolved. Pour into caramelized pans. Place flan pan or pie pans into larger pan filled with water.

Bake in preheated 350° oven for 1 hour. Cool and refrigerate.

Mix raspberries with 2 tablespoons of Chambord and let sit for 1 hour.

Invert custards onto plate. Cut into 8 pieces. Drizzle raspberries on top of each serving.

Amaretto Freeze

Serves one generously.

2	scoops vanilla ice cream
1½	ounces Amaretto
½	ounce Crème de Cacao
	splash half and half
	small handful of ice

Blend until creamy smooth.

Pour into chilled glasses. Serve.

Raspberry Crème Brulée

Serves 6

12	ounces frozen unsweetened raspberries, thawed and drained
¾	cup sugar, divided
2	teaspoons raspberry liqueur
5	egg yolks
2	cups whipping cream
¼	teaspoon vanilla extract
5	tablespoons butter, unsalted
⅓	cup brown sugar, firmly packed

Toss berries gently in bowl with ¼ cup sugar and liqueur. Divide berries among six ¾ cup, broiler–proof custard cups.

In heavy saucepan, whisk egg yolks and add remaining ½ cup sugar until pale and thick, about three minutes. Add cream and vanilla. Set sauce pan over medium heat. Stir until custard thickens and leaves path on back of spoon when finger is drawn across, about 7 minutes. Do not boil. Add butter and stir until melted.

Spoon over berries carefully. Cover and refrigerate at least 4 hours or overnight.

Preheat broiler. Press brown sugar through sieve over custards. Broil until sugar begins to melt and caramelize, about 2 minutes.

Chill for 3 hours before serving.

Orange Pancakes

Serves 8

2	eggs, beaten
2	cups whipping cream
4	6–ounce cans frozen orange juice concentrate, divided
2	cups pancake mix
1	cup butter
2	cups sugar

Add beaten eggs, cream and ½ cup frozen orange juice to pancake mix. Stir well and bake on greased hot griddle. Serve with orange sauce.

Place remaining orange juice, butter and sugar in saucepan to make sauce. Simmer until desired thickness.

Spoon sauce over pancakes and serve.

Apple, Apricot and Raisin Cobbler

Serves 10 to 12

¼	pound butter

Fruit mixture:

3½	cups canned cooked apples
1½	cups dried apricots
¾	cup raisins
1	cup brown sugar
1	teaspoon cinnamon

Batter:

2½	cups sugar
½	teaspoon salt
2½	teaspoons baking powder
1¾	cups flour
1¾	cups milk

Mix fruit, sugar and cinnamon together. Set aside.

Melt butter in 9 x 13–inch cake pan.

Mix batter ingredients in bowl. Beat in milk until lumps are gone. Pour batter into melted butter. Do not stir. Spoon fruit mixture over the top of the batter. Do not stir.

Bake 95 minutes in 350° oven or until top is brown. Serve with whipped cream.

Surprise Meringues

Yields 24

The surprise is chocolate!

2	egg whites
⅛	teaspoon salt
⅛	teaspoon vanilla
⅓	teaspoon cream of tartar
¾	cup sugar
1	6–ounce package semisweet tiny chocolate chips
¼	cup pecans, crushed

Beat egg whites, salt, cream of tartar and vanilla until soft peaks form. Add sugar gradually, beating until stiff. Fold in chocolate pieces and nuts.

Drop by rounded teaspoon onto cookie sheet lined with brown paper.

Bake at 300° for 25 minutes.

Etceteras

A good kitchen is a good apothecaries shop.

—William Bulletin

Minnesota Muesli

Serves 10

Healthy and hearty way to start the day!

2	cups rolled oats
½	cup walnuts, coarsely chopped
½	cup raisins
½	cup tart apple, chopped
½	cup brown sugar
1	teaspoon cinnamon
1	quart whipping cream or half and half

Mix ingredients well.

Refrigerate for at least 15 hours before serving.

Goat Cheese Croutons

Yields 16 pieces

Excellent with salads or soups.

½	baguette
3	tablespoons olive oil
3	ounces goat cheese

Slice baguette into ½ inch pieces. Brush with olive oil. Bake at 400° for 15 minutes, or until lightly browned.

Spread with goat cheese and run under broiler briefly.

Place croutons in center of plate. Serve with *Greens with Basil Vinaigrette.

Yogurt Cheese

Delicious, low–fat alternative to cream cheese and wonderful on bagels.

1	carton non-fat yogurt with no gelatin in ingredients
1	strainer
	cheesecloth
	plastic wrap or foil

Place yogurt in cheesecloth covered strainer and place over bowl. Cover with plastic or foil and refrigerate for 2 to 24 hours. The longer yogurt drains the thicker the cheese.

Discard whey and refrigerate cheese in covered container.

May flavor with jam, honey, cinnamon–sugar, onion, herbs or anything you choose.

Freezer Raspberry Jam

Yields 1 quart

Simple and delicious!

1	quart fresh raspberries, ripened
3	cups sugar, divided
½	teaspoon butter

Place berries in colander and pour boiling water over them. Place in saucepan with 2 cups sugar and butter. Boil 2 minutes. Add remaining sugar and boil 5 minutes.

Let stand at room temperature in shallow dish for 2 days covered with plastic wrap. Put in sterilized glass jars and freeze.

Butter prevents the formation of film on top.

Lemon Curd Jam

A recipe from my pen–pal of 44 years from South Devon, England.

Wonderful on scones or toast!

	rind and juice of 3 large lemons
8	ounces sugar
3	eggs, well beaten
4	ounces margarine

Grate off rind of lemons and squeeze out juice. Place in top of double boiler with the sugar and margarine. Cook until ingredients are melted.

Add beaten eggs and continue cooking until the mixture coats the back of wooden spoon.

Pour into jars and refrigerate.

Cranberry Wine Jelly

Yields 5 half–pint jars

This makes a lovely hostess gift at holiday time.

2	cups cranberry juice
3½	cups sugar
3	ounces liquid fruit pectin
¼	cup port wine

Combine cranberry juice and sugar in 4–quart saucepan. Bring to boil, stirring constantly. Stir in pectin and bring back to a rolling boil. Boil hard for 1 minute. Remove from heat and stir in wine. Skim off any foam.

Ladle into hot, sterilized jars. Seal with thin film of paraffin.

Cranberry Chutney

Sweet holiday gift idea.

1	pound cranberries
1	cup granulated sugar
½	cup maple syrup
1 ½	teaspoons ground ginger
¼	teaspoon ground allspice
½	cup golden raisins
1	cup water
2	teaspoons ground cinnamon
½	teaspoon ground cloves
1	cup onion, chopped
1	cup apple, chopped
½	cup celery, chopped

Simmer cranberries, sugar, syrup, raisins, water and spices, uncovered, over medium heat about 15 minutes.

Stir in onion, apple and celery. Simmer until thick, approximately 15 minutes.

Will keep several weeks in refrigerator.

Indian Chutney

Yields 2 cups

Serve with Quick Tandoori Chicken* or any grilled meat.

10–12	garlic cloves, peeled
¼	cup fresh ginger, peeled and chopped
1½	cups red wine vinegar
1	16–ounce can plum tomatoes, including juice
1½	cups sugar
½	teaspoon pepper, freshly ground
½	teaspoon salt
½	cup golden raisins
½	cup almonds or walnuts
½	teaspoon cayenne or to taste

Purée garlic and ginger with vinegar in food processor. Combine tomatoes and juice with purée in non–reactive pan. Add sugar, salt and pepper. Bring to boil and simmer until reduced, stirring constantly.

Reduce to a simmer until chutney thickens, 2 to 3 hours, depending on level of heat.

Add raisins, nuts and cayenne. Heat until raisins are hot. Cool and serve at room temperature.

Zucchini and Lime Relish

2	medium limes, thinly sliced and then chopped
3	medium zucchini, peeled and shredded
½	cup lime juice
¼	cup cider vinegar
¼	teaspoon salt
1¾	ounces fruit pectin
4	cups sugar

Combine limes, zucchini, lime juice, vinegar and salt in 5–quart saucepan. Stir thoroughly. Add fruit pectin.

Bring to fast boil. Stir in sugar and boil 1 minute.

Remove from heat. Stir with wooden spoon for 5 minutes. Ladle into sterilized, hot canning jars and seal.

Store in refrigerator.

Cranberry Salsa

1	12–ounce package fresh cranberries, washed and drained
4	oranges, diced
2	mangoes, diced
½	cup cilantro, chopped
1	tablespoon fresh ginger, grated
1	teaspoon fresh thyme
2–3	tablespoons honey
1	teaspoon fresh rosemary
½	teaspoon cinnamon
¼	teaspoon ground cloves
¼	cup (scant) fresh lime juice

Chop cranberries in food processor. Combine all ingredients. Taste to determine if additional honey is needed for sweetness.

Salsa, in Spanish, means a sauce usually made with tomatoes and peppers. Americans have broadened their salsas to include many fresh fruits and vegetables.

Quick Cream Fish Sauce

Serves 6

Especially good with salmon!

¼	cup dry white wine
1	cup sour cream
¼	cup mayonnaise
8	teaspoons dill
1	tablespoon onion, minced
2	tablespoons green pepper, minced
½	teaspoon salt

Stir wine into sour cream and add remaining ingredients. Blend well. Refrigerate for several hours to ensure blending of flavors.

Serve over baked, broiled or fried fish.

Tri–Color Pepper Sauce

Serves 6

Good with firm, fresh fish.

1	each green, yellow and red pepper, cut into diamond shapes or cubed very small
4	tablespoons fresh ginger, grated
5	garlic cloves, minced
3	tablespoons fresh cilantro, chopped
2	tablespoons butter

Sauté all ingredients lightly for about 5 minutes.

Serve over grilled salmon steak or fillet.

Secret Sauce

Excellent with seafood or pork ribs!

½	pound butter
¼	cup soy sauce
¼	cup ketchup
2	tablespoons prepared mustard
	Worcestershire sauce to taste
	hickory smoked salt to taste

Combine all ingredients in saucepan. Simmer for 15 minutes.

Serve warm with seafood.

Herb Sauce

Yields 2½ cups

Excellent with cold chicken, salmon or paté!

2	shallots, chopped
4	garlic cloves, minced
½	cup parsley, chopped
1	cup mayonnaise
½	cup sour cream
⅓	cup fresh lemon juice
½	teaspoon each:
	thyme
	rosemary
	sage
	basil
	marjoram
	tarragon
	oregano
	dill
¼	cup olive oil
¼	cup sherry
	salt and pepper to taste

Combine shallots, garlic, parsley, mayonnaise, sour cream, lemon juice and herbs. Blend thoroughly until sauce is very smooth.

Add oil in steady stream. Add sherry, salt and pepper, if desired.

Watercress Sauce

Yields 2 cups

Wonderful on salmon or any other seafood.

1	cup mayonnaise
1	cup watercress
½	cup chives
2	tablespoons olive oil
2	tablespoons lemon juice
1	tablespoon parsley
3	anchovies
½	teaspoon salt
¼	teaspoon white pepper
½	cup sour cream

Combine all ingredients, except sour cream, in blender.

Add sour cream and mix well.

Red Pesto Sauce

Yields 1½ cups

½ cup oil–packed sun–dried tomatoes, drained and chopped
3 cups fresh basil, loosely packed
3 garlic cloves
½ cup Romano cheese, freshly grated
½ cup walnuts
½ cup olive oil, divided
½ teaspoon salt
¼ teaspoon pepper, freshly ground

Process sun–dried tomatoes with basil and garlic in food processor, pulsing motor until mixture is coarsely chopped. Add cheese, nuts and ¼ cup oil. Process for 10 seconds. Add remaining oil, salt and pepper while motor is running. Scrape the side of processor bowl and process until well combined.

Pesto Sauce

2 cups fresh basil
    or
1 cup basil and 1 cup parsley, stripped from stems
1 teaspoon salt
½ teaspoon black pepper
1 garlic clove, pressed
2 tablespoons pine nuts or walnuts
½ cup Parmesan cheese, grated
½ cup olive oil

Combine basil, salt, pepper, garlic and pine nuts in blender. Add cheese. Add oil gradually, as blender runs, to make a smooth paste.

Ham Sauce

Yields 1 pint

½ cup prepared mustard
½ cup tomato soup
½ cup vinegar
½ cup sugar (scant)
½ cup butter
2 egg yolks, well–beaten

Cook all ingredients, except egg yolks, in double boiler.

Just before serving, add egg yolks and stir until thickened. Serve hot.

Greatest Mustard Sauce

Yields 2 cups

Excellent with ham!

1	cup granulated sugar
1	rounded tablespoon dry mustard
¾	cup cider vinegar
¼	cup water
3	eggs, beaten

Mix sugar and mustard together in saucepan. Add vinegar and water slowly to mixture. Add eggs and cook, stirring constantly, until sauce thickens, about 10 to 15 minutes.

Serve hot or cold.

Sauce may be frozen and it will store refrigerated for a month.

Mustard Sauce

Yields 1¼ cup

1	cup mayonnaise
1	tablespoon olive oil
1	tablespoon lemon juice
1	tablespoon dry mustard
1	tablespoon A–1 Sauce
2	teaspoons Worcestershire sauce
1	dash cayenne pepper
⅛	teaspoon salt

Mix mustard with lemon juice. Add oil, A–1 Sauce, Worcestershire, salt and cayenne. Mix well.

Add mixture to mayonnaise and mix until thoroughly combined.

Mint Mustard Sauce

Yields 1 cup

Wonderful served with fish, ham, pork or lamb.

1¼	tablespoons Dijon mustard
1¼	tablespoons coarse–grained mustard
3	tablespoons wine vinegar
¼	cup fresh mint leaves, firmly packed
¾	cup olive oil

Blend together mustards, vinegar and mint. Add oil in steady stream while motor is running and blend until emulsified.

Basic Hollandaise

Yields 1 cup

An extra egg yolk makes this a thick hollandaise.

4	egg yolks
2	tablespoons lemon juice
½	teaspoon salt
	dash cayenne pepper
½	cup unsalted butter

Place egg yolks, lemon juice, salt and cayenne in food processor bowl. Using knife blade, process until smooth, about 3 seconds.

Pour in bubbling melted butter a small amount at a time while still processing. It is essential that the butter is bubbling or sauce will not thicken. Process until smooth.

Keep warm in double boiler. Do not allow sauce to boil or curdle.

 We urge our readers to consider the possible danger of serving eggs that have not been completely cooked.

Sauce Maltaise

Yields 1 cup

Excellent on fresh asparagus.

1	tablespoon orange juice
1	teaspoon lemon juice
	peel from large orange, grated
1	cup Basic Hollandaise*

Add ingredients to hollandaise. Mix well and serve.

Cucumbers in Sour Cream

Serves 4 to 6

A nice accompaniment for a casual fête.

1	16–ounce carton sour cream
¼	cup apple cider vinegar
¼	cup sugar or more to taste
	salt and pepper to taste
1–2	cucumbers, thinly sliced
1	sweet onion, thinly sliced and separated

Mix sour cream, vinegar and sugar in bowl. Add cucumbers and onions.

Stir and refrigerate.

Murphy–Goode Cabernet Sauvignon Dipping Sauce

Compliments your Oriental appetizers.

½	cup Murphy–Goode Cabernet Sauvignon
1	tablespoon soy sauce
1	tablespoon white rice vinegar
½	tablespoon sesame oil
1	green onion, finely sliced into rings

Reduce Murphy–Goode Cabernet Sauvignon in half. Mix with remaining ingredients and garnish with green onions.

Seasoned Salt

Wonderful for roasting fowl or at the grill.

1	tablespoon salt
½	teaspoon pepper, freshly ground
½	teaspoon granulated garlic
½	teaspoon allspice
1	teaspoon sugar
	cayenne pepper

Mix ingredients well.

Ben's Guaranteed Steak Preparation Secret

Guaranteed to be high in sodium and fat, but the taste is worth an occasional splurge!

lemon pepper
garlic salt
soy sauce
olive oil

Rub into both sides of steak or hamburger patty generous amounts of the ingredients in order of listing.

Cook quickly over hot charcoal fire, slightly charring meat.

Mom's Foamy Sauce

Yields 2 cups

Outstanding on plum pudding!

2	eggs, separated
1	cup powdered sugar
½	cup butter, softened
1	cup heavy cream, whipped
	brandy to taste

Beat egg whites until very stiff. Set aside.

Cream sugar and butter together in top of double boiler. Add egg yolks and beat until creamy. Place double boiler over heat. Stir mixture constantly until it is melted and slightly thick. Remove from heat and gently fold in egg whites. Let sauce rest on back of stove until ready to serve.

Whip cream. Fold into sauce just before serving. Add brandy to taste and ladle over steaming pudding.

Prune Sauce

Excellent with roast pork!

1	pound prunes
2	tablespoons sugar
2	teaspoons lemon zest
¼	cup water
½	cup port

Cook prunes. Remove pits and purée in food processor or push through sieve. Add sugar and lemon zest to purée.

Cook with water over low heat for 10 minutes. Add port and bring sauce to boil. Remove from heat and serve.

Orange–Yogurt Dip

Yields 1 cup

1	8–ounce carton plain low–fat yogurt
2	tablespoons honey
	peel of ½ orange, grated

Combine ingredients in a small bowl. Chill.

Serve as dip for orange sections or slices of apple or banana or serve over cut–up fruit or berries.

Chocolate Sauce

Yields 1 cup

Use on ice cream, cake or frozen yogurt.

1	square chocolate
1	tablespoon butter or margarine
½	cup boiling water
1	cup sugar
2	tablespoons corn syrup
½	teaspoon vanilla
	pinch salt

Melt chocolate over hot water. Add butter and melt. Slowly add boiling water and mix well. Bring to boil. Remove from heat

Add sugar and corn syrup. Put back on burner and boil, gently, for 5 minutes. Remove from heat, cool and add vanilla and salt.

Worth–the–Calories Hot Fudge Sauce

¼	pound butter
1½	cups dark brown sugar, packed
¼	cup white sugar
1	cup half and half
¾	cup Droste cocoa

Melt butter in skillet. Add remaining ingredients and simmer fifteen minutes.

Serve over peppermint, coffee or vanilla ice cream.

English Toffee

1	pound butter
2	cups sugar
9	ounces chocolate chips
¾	cup nuts, chopped

Melt chocolate chips in double boiler and keep warm.

Melt butter in heavy skillet over hot fire. Stir in sugar with wooden spoon, stirring constantly until mixture turns toffee colored and candy thermometer reaches 300°.

Pour into greased, 11 x 14–inch jelly roll pan. Spread with chocolate mixture. Sprinkle with nuts. Cool and break into pieces.

Burt's Favorite Short–Cut Fudge

Yields 64 small squares

3	squares bitter chocolate
1	cup condensed milk
1½	tablespoons butter, softened
1	teaspoon vanilla
2	cups powdered sugar, sifted
1	cup pecans, chopped

Melt chocolate in top of double boiler. Add condensed milk. Cook 5 minutes, stirring occasionally, until mixture thickens. Remove from heat.

Add butter and vanilla. Mix well. Add sifted sugar carefully to chocolate mixture. Fold in nuts. Pour into buttered brownie pan.

Place in refrigerator until thoroughly chilled. Cut into squares.

Chocolate Truffles

Yields 3 to 4 dozen candies

⅔	cup heavy cream
3	tablespoons butter, cut into chunks
2	tablespoons sugar
2	4–ounce packages German sweet chocolate, broken
	unsweetened cocoa
	angel flaked coconut, optional
	crushed nuts, optional

Bring cream, butter and sugar to full boil over medium heat, stirring constantly. Remove from heat. Add chocolate and continue stirring until chocolate is melted and mixture is smooth.

Chill until firm enough to handle, about 3½ hours.

Shape into ½ inch balls. Roll in cocoa. Roll chocolate balls into angel flaked softened coconut or crushed nuts, if desired.

Place waxed paper liners between each layer of chocolate balls when storing. Store covered truffles in refrigerator.

Truffles with Grand Marnier

Yields 1 dozen

They freeze well!

⅓	cup whipping cream
8	ounces semi–sweet chocolate, broken into pieces
1	tablespoon Grand Marnier
¼	cup Dutch cocoa

Heat cream in small heavy saucepan until it bubbles. Remove from heat and add chocolate. Stir to combine. Cover first with paper towel, then with lid or plate.

Let stand 5 minutes.

Stir gently until chocolate has combined with cream. Stir in Grand Marnier. Beat with electric beater until mixture becomes light and fluffy. Refrigerate a few minutes. Beat again until mixture changes color.

Remove portions the size of large marbles and roll quickly between your palms. Roll in cocoa to coat well and place in frilled candy cup.

❧ *Truffles were so named because the original cocoa–coated and rather misshapen confection resembled the famous and rare fungus of the same name.*

Coconut–Pecan Frosting

1	cup evaporated milk
1	cup sugar
3	egg yolks
½	cup butter
1	teaspoon vanilla
1	square bitter chocolate
⅓	cup coconut, chopped
⅓	cup pecans, chopped

Combine all ingredients except coconut and pecans. Cook over medium heat until smooth, about 12 minutes. Add coconut and pecans.

Superb on German chocolate cake or as glaze for pre–packaged miniature cinnamon rolls.

Grandmother West's Hot Spiced Tea

Grandmother was famous in Athens, Georgia, for this refreshing drink!

8	cups water, divided
2	teaspoons instant tea
¾	cup sugar
¼	cup Tang
½	cup lemon juice, fresh or reconstituted
2	tablespoons whole cloves

Boil cloves in 2 cups of water for 5 minutes. Remove cloves and reserve water.

Bring 6 cups of water to boil. Add tea, sugar, Tang, lemon juice and water from cloves. Let stand, covered, for several minutes and serve.

Cafe Vienna

A great holiday gift!

⅔	cup instant coffee
2	cups instant nonfat dry milk
4	tablespoons nonfat dairy creamer
1	cup powdered sugar
½	cup instant hot chocolate drink mix
½	teaspoon cinnamon

Mix ingredients well and store in an air tight container. To use, mix 2 heaping teaspoons per cup of boiling water.

Glüee

Delicious holiday drink!

1	cup sugar
½	cup water
10	cloves
3	cinnamon sticks
2	strips lemon peel
1	750 ml bottle red wine

Make a syrup of sugar, water, cloves, cinnamon and lemon peel. Strain and add red wine.

Serve warm to holiday guests.

Syrup can be made in advance and added before serving.

Texas Milk Punch

This is the traditional New Year's Day drink in Texas instead of eggnog!

1	gallon milk
⅔	cup sugar
1	liter Kentucky bourbon
½	ounce creme de cocoa
3	dashes vanilla extract
	nutmeg

Pour milk into large container. Add sugar and stir until sugar dissolves completely. Add bourbon and stir. Add creme de cacao and stir again. Stir in vanilla extract. Keep chilled in refrigerator until ready to serve.

Serve in tumbler with nutmeg sprinkled on top.

Great Non–Alcoholic Punch

Serves 25 to 30 people

3	quarts ginger–ale
1	10–ounce can frozen orange juice
1	10–ounce can frozen lemonade
1	quart pineapple sherbet
1	quart 1% milk

Mix all ingredients together well.

Refrigerate.

Cadillac Bar's Ramos Gin Fizz

Serves 1

1	ounce dry gin
	juice of 1 lemon
1	teaspoon powdered sugar
1	egg white
3	ounces whipping cream
6	drops orange flower water

Mix all ingredients in blender.

Serve over crushed ice in a tall glass.

Chefs & Culinary Consultants

Cooking is one of the arts, and the basis of all art is discipline.

—Voltaire

Black and White Bean Soup
with Red Jalapeño Sour Cream

Serves 16

Yields 1 gallon

Red Jalapeño Sour Cream:

1	cup sour cream
3	red jalapeños, seeded and chopped
1	teaspoon lime juice
	salt and white pepper to taste

Purée all ingredients in blender until smooth and homogenous in color.

Cover and refrigerate until ready to use.

White Bean Soup:

2	tablespoons corn oil
1	onion, peeled and chopped
3	cloves garlic, minced
2	ribs celery, chopped
1	bay leaf
1	teaspoon fresh thyme, chopped
½	teaspoon white pepper
½	teaspoon coriander seeds
1	teaspoon cumin
2	cups white wine
8	cups homemade chicken stock
	or
	canned chicken broth
1	ham bone
3	cups navy beans, soaked overnight
1	cup heavy cream
1	cup half and half
	salt and white pepper to taste

In a gallon stock pot, heat oil and add onion, garlic and celery. Sauté until onion is translucent and add remaining ingredients. Bring to a boil and simmer until beans are soft, about 45 minutes. Remove ham bone from soup and purée soup in batches in a blender. Pass soup through a strainer and season with salt and white pepper. Reheat and hold until ready to serve.

continued from page 234

Black Bean Soup:
½	pound bacon, diced
1	medium onion, peeled and chopped
2	cloves garlic, minced
2	red bell peppers, seeded and chopped
1	teaspoon cumin
1	teaspoon oregano
1	teaspoon whole cloves
1	bay leaf
1	teaspoon fresh thyme
2	cups dry sherry
2	cups tomatoes, seeded and diced
2	tablespoons cilantro, stemmed and chopped
10	cups homemade beef or veal stock
	or
	canned broth with no salt
3	cups black beans, sorted and soaked overnight

In a gallon stock pot, render fat from bacon and add onion, peppers and tomato. Cook until onion is translucent. Add remaining ingredients and simmer until beans are soft, about 30 minutes. In batches, purée soup in blender and pass through a strainer. Adjust seasoning with salt and pepper. Reheat and hold until ready to serve.

Using 2 ladles, simultaneously pour white and black bean soups, side by side, into bowls. Using a tablespoon, drizzle *Red Pepper Jalapeño Sour Cream over each soup serving.

Mark Haugen
Tejas
Cuisine of the Southwest

Seafood Cakes with Pasilla–Corn Relish and Tomato–Vinaigrette

Serves 8 to 10

Seafood Cakes:

1	tablespoon each minced celery, carrots and onion
1	tablespoon each red and green bell pepper, seeded and minced
1	tablespoon jalapeño pepper, seeded and minced
1	teaspoon garlic, minced
½	pound shrimp
½	pound scallops
½	pound any firm white fish, such as snapper or halibut, finely chopped
½	teaspoon each fresh basil, thyme and rosemary chopped
½	teaspoon cumin
½	teaspoon white pepper
1	teaspoon dry mustard
1	teaspoon salt
½	teaspoon coriander, ground
	juice of 1 lime
1	egg
	whole chives

In a large bowl, combine all ingredients thoroughly. Form 2-ounce balls and shape into patties, allowing for two patties per person.

In a large skillet, heat 4 tablespoons butter and cook seafood patties about 4 minutes per side. Meanwhile, drizzle *Tomato–Vinaigrette on each plate, add a dollop of sour cream and cover with 2 tablespoons of *Pasilla–Corn Relish. Arrange two seafood cakes on each plate, garnish with 2 whole chives and serve.

Pasilla–Corn Relish

6	ears corn, grilled on charcoal grill for 15 to 20 minutes, or until nicely browned
2	dried pasilla chilies, soaked in hot water until soft, seeded and julienned
3	tablespoons chives, minced
	juice of 1 lime
¾	teaspoon salt

When corn cools, cut niblets from ear and combine with remaining ingredients.

Refrigerate.

Tomato–Vinaigrette

5	ripe tomatoes, cut in half, seeded and grilled over hickory chips for 20 to 30 minutes
4	tablespoons shallots, minced
½	cup red wine vinegar
1	tablespoon tomato paste
1	teaspoon salt
½	teaspoon white pepper
1	cup virgin olive oil
1	cup corn oil

In a blender combine tomatoes, shallots, vinegar, tomato paste, salt and pepper. Blend, using progressively faster speeds, until tomatoes are puréed. Slowly add olive and corn oils.

Refrigerate.

Mark Haugen
Tejas
Cuisine of the Southwest

Chilled Saffron Scallops with Basil Mayonnaise

Serves 8

1	quart strong fish stock
1	pound bay scallops
4–5	threads saffron

Mayonnaise:

1	cup fresh mayonnaise
1	tablespoon fresh basil, chopped
	Bibb lettuce leaves
8	ounces spinach leaves, julienned
16	wedges of tomato

Heat fish stock and infuse saffron. Stock will turn yellow. As stock comes to a simmer, add scallops and poach for a minute or two. Remove from heat and cool scallops in liquid used to poach.

For mayonnaise, blend fresh mayonnaise with chopped basil and blend well.

To assemble dish, place Bibb lettuce on plate. Place spinach in center of lettuce, spreading it out in a 3–inch circle, and top with cooled scallops. Garnish with tomato wedges.

Western International Hotels

Grilled Vegetable Salad with Queso Fresco and Red Pepper Vinaigrette

Serves 4

Vinaigrette:

1	red pepper, roasted, peeled and seeded
4	ounces red wine vinegar
1	shallot, peeled
1	teaspoon salt
½	teaspoon white pepper
¾	cup extra virgin olive oil
¾	cup corn oil

Place bell pepper, vinegar, shallot, salt and white pepper in a blender and purée until smooth. Slowly blend in the 2 oils.

Refrigerate. Extra vinaigrette may be saved up to one week.

Grilled Vegetables:

¼	cup corn oil
1	zucchini, ¼ inch thick slices
1	yellow squash, ¼ inch thick slices
1	avocado, ¼ inch thick slices
1	each red, yellow and green pepper, seeded and cut into triangle shapes
4	scallions
1	tomato, ¼ inch thick slices
2	ears corn, grilled and cut into niblets

Light charcoal fire and lightly salt and oil vegetables. When coals are white hot, lay vegetables, except tomatoes, on grill and cook for 2 minutes on each side. Cook tomatoes for 30 seconds on each side. Spoon 3 ounces vinaigrette onto each plate and arrange vegetables on top of vinaigrette. Sprinkle with 1 tablespoon queso fresco, which may be purchased at specialty Mexican stores.

Serve with salsa and tortillas.

Mark Haugen
Tejas
Cuisine of the Southwest

Sautéed Atlantic Salmon with Fennel Consommé

Yields 2 cups

Fennel Consommé:

1	quart chicken consommé
½	teaspoon saffron threads
2	ounces Pernod
2	ounces dry white wine
½	pound chopped fennel
2–3	garlic cloves
1	bouquet garni with thyme, bay leaf, peppercorn, etc.

Salmon:

1	6–ounce salmon fillet, boned, skin and belly fat removed
	sea salt and white pepper
	clarified butter for cooking
2	ounces fennel, julienned and blanched
4	ounces fennel consommé
1	tablespoon unsalted butter
½	tablespoon fennel tops, chopped
½	ounce Pernod
1	6–inch fry pan
1	3-inch fry pan
	fennel sprigs for garnish

Combine all ingredients in consommé. Simmer until aromatic. Strain through bouillon strainer or cheesecloth.

Salt and pepper salmon fillet. Heat frying pan and add clarified butter. When pan is smoking hot, add salmon fillet, flesh side down. Cook until well caramelized, turn over and cook in a 450° oven.

Meanwhile, burn off Pernod in 3–inch fry pan. Add fennel consommé and julienned fennel. Reduce to one half. Remove from heat, add unsalted butter and fennel tops. Correct seasonings.

Paint dinner plates with sauce and place salmon fillet on top of sauce. Garnish with fresh fennel.

Jack Stalcar
Woodhill Country Club

Chicken Hash à la Cookery

Serves 10 to 12

2	pounds boned chicken meat
	flour for dusting
1	tablespoon each butter and oil
1	large onion, finely chopped
1	red pepper, finely chopped
2	large red potatoes, boiled and diced
1	10–ounce package frozen corn nuggets
1	10–ounce package frozen chopped spinach, drained well
1	teaspoon jalapeño pepper, chopped
¾	cup chicken broth
¼	cup heavy cream or crème fraîche
¼	cup Parmesan cheese
	salt and pepper
1	tablespoon fresh basil, chopped

Garnishes:

    guacamole
    sour cream
    chopped olives
    scallions

Lay chicken meat on a cookie sheet and put in freezer. When meat is firm, but not frozen, remove to a cutting board. Dip in flour to lightly dust and dice.

Heat butter and oil in a large skillet. Sauté chicken on medium–high heat until golden, but not overcooked. Remove from pan and reserve.

Add onion and more butter, if necessary. Cook 5 minutes. Add pepper and potatoes. Cook another 5 minutes. Stir in corn, jalapeño peppers and chopped spinach. Cook to heat through.

Combine broth, cream and Parmesan cheese. Stir into hash with reserved chicken and cook about 5 minutes. Season with salt and pepper. Sprinkle with basil.

Serve with garnishes.

Recipe may be prepared early and reheated. It also freezes well.

Sara Monick
The Cookery

Peking Turkey

Serves 10

12–14	pound turkey
8	cups water
⅓	cup honey
3	tablespoons hoisin sauce
1½	tablespoons bean sauce
2	tablespoons soy sauce
1	tablespoon Chinese five spice
1	bunch fresh coriander (cilantro)
1	bunch green onions
1	small bunch celery

Defrost turkey if frozen. Remove neck and giblets. Rinse turkey and place breast side down on a roasting rack set in the sink. Heat water and honey to boiling; slowly pour about half of the liquid over the exposed side of the turkey. Turn bird over and pour remaining liquid over breast side. Place uncovered in refrigerator overnight.

Meanwhile, mix hoisin sauce, bean sauce, soy sauce and Chinese five spice. Rinse coriander and cut off stem ends. Clean green onions and celery. Cut onions and celery into bite–sized pieces.

Remove turkey from refrigerator; generously rub sauce mixture inside body and neck cavities. Stuff cavities with onions, celery and coriander. Fasten neck skin to back with skewer. Leave wings and legs untied. Place turkey on rack in roasting pan.

Roast turkey, breast side up, at 350° for about 12 minutes per pound or until a meat thermometer inserted in thickest portion registers 185°. Baste with pan juices several times during roasting. Remove turkey from oven and transfer to cutting board or platter. Remove stuffing vegetables and moisten with any accumulated juices from inside the bird.

Two whole chickens or ducks may be substituted for the turkey.

Joanne Topp
Sue Zelickson

Southwestern Turkey Breast with Stuffing

Serves 4

2-3	pound turkey breast
3	tablespoons olive oil
¼	teaspoon cayenne pepper
¼	teaspoon cumin
¼	teaspoon ground sage
¼	teaspoon cinnamon

Rub turkey breast with oil, then rub in other ingredients. Roast at 350° for 2 hours.

Serve with *Southwestern Stuffing, sautéed bell peppers and flour tortillas.

Southwestern Stuffing

¼	cup olive oil
¼	cup pecans
1	small onion, diced
1	tablespoon garlic, crushed
2–3	cups chicken stock
1	teaspoon cumin
1	teaspoon ground sage
1	teaspoon celery salt
1	small can jalapeño peppers
1½	pounds corn bread, crumbled
1½	pounds whole wheat bread, cubed
2	eggs beaten
1	cup milk

Heat olive oil over medium heat. Add pecans, onion and garlic. Sauté 3 to 4 minutes. Add chicken stock and seasonings.

Place corn bread and wheat bread in bowl. Pour pecan mixture over bread and mix. Add eggs. If a little dry, add milk or more chicken stock.

Put in baking dish and bake at 350° for 45 minutes.

Peter Metzger
Radisson Plaza Hotel

Caribbean Turkey with Pineapple Salsa

Serves 4

2-3½	pound turkey breast
3	tablespoons butter
¾	cup honey
½	cup lime juice
	salt and pepper to taste
¾	teaspoon nutmeg
½	cup lemon juice

Place turkey in roasting pan. Salt and pepper to taste. Bake at 350° for 2 hours. Combine remaining ingredients in small sauce pan. Stir until blended. Brush on turkey as it is roasting.

Serve with *Pineapple Salsa.

Pineapple Salsa

2½	cups fresh or canned pineapple, diced
2	green onions, diced
1	green pepper, diced
1	red pepper, diced
1	tablespoon cilantro, chopped
3	tablespoons orange juice

Combine all ingredients. Let stand 2 to 3 hours to blend flavors.

Serve with *Caribbean Turkey.

Peter Metzger
Radisson Plaza Hotel

Explore the exotic fruits at your local markets. Try mango, kumquat, carambola (star fruit), guava, papaya or passion fruit to create your own salsa.

Crespelle with Ham and Green Peas and Salsa Balsamella

Serves 8

Crespelle:

½	cup cold water
½	cup milk
2	eggs
¼	teaspoon salt
1	cup all–purpose flour, sifted
2	tablespoons melted butter
2	tablespoons butter, in one chunk
	small square cheesecloth

Place water, milk, eggs, salt and flour in bowl of blender. Blend to combine. Add melted butter and blend once more. Refrigerate at least 2 hours. Strain before using.

Heat a 6–inch crêpe pan to moderate heat. Wrap chunk of butter in cheesecloth and swab the bottom of the pan. Add 2 to 3 tablespoons of crêpe batter, tilting pan until the bottom is evenly covered. Cook until the wet look has disappeared, then turn crêpe with metal spatula and continue to cook 1 minute. Turn out on kitchen towel, stacking one on top of another until all are done. Makes 16.

Salsa Balsamella:

6	tablespoons butter
2	shallots, finely minced
6	tablespoons flour
1	teaspoon salt
	several gratings of nutmeg
3	cups milk, warmed

Heat butter in sauce pan. Sauté shallots until softened. Add flour.

Cook, stirring frequently, for one minute without browning. Season with salt, white pepper and nutmeg. Add the heated milk. Whisk until smooth. Divide in half.

¾	pound high quality baked ham, diced
1	cup frozen tiny peas, blanched and drained

Into half of the Salsa Balsamella, stir the ham and peas. Fill the crêpes with about 3 tablespoons of mixture and roll up. Place two filled crêpes into each of 8 individual buttered au gratin dishes.

½	cup Parmesan cheese, grated

To finish, mask the crêpes with remaining Salsa Balsamella. Top with grated Parmesan cheese. Bake at 350° for 15 to 18 minutes.

Marion Conlin

Crostini of Almonds and Pine Nuts

Sweet Tarte Pastry:
- ½ cup butter
- ½ cup sugar
- 1½ cups flour
- 2 egg yolks
- 1 teaspoon vanilla

Crostini:
- 1 recipe Sweet Tarte Pastry
- ½ cup slivered almonds
- ¾ cup granulated sugar
- ½ cup butter, softened
- 3 whole eggs, slightly beaten
- 2 tablespoons lemon juice
- 1 cup pine nuts

Prepare tarte pastry by combining butter, sugar and flour in food processor. With processor running, pour egg yolks and vanilla through feed tube. Process to combine. Press into prepared 10–inch tarte tin. Bake at 375° for 12 to 15 minutes.

Place almonds in bowl of food processor. Add sugar. Process to grind almonds well. Add butter, eggs and lemon juice. Process to blend. Pour into pre–baked shell. Scatter pine nuts evenly over the surface. Cover with foil tent.

Bake at 350° for 45 minutes. Remove cover and continue to bake until top is nicely browned.

Cool to room temperature before serving.

Marion Conlin
Home Kitchen Cooking School

ᱚ *In Italy, crostini are often served as a midmorning*
or afternoon snack, rather than as dessert. They are
delicious accompanied by a cup of cappuccino or a
glass of sweet wine.

Chicken Dijonnaise

Serves 4

4	8–ounce chicken breasts, boned and skinned
	salt and pepper to taste
4	tablespoons Dijon mustard
2	cups fresh white breadcrumbs
¼	cup clarified butter
2	cups heavy cream
2	tablespoons Dijon mustard

Season chicken breasts with salt and pepper. Brush top of breast with Dijon mustard. Dip into bread crumbs and refrigerate ½ hour, if possible.

Pour clarified butter into hot sauté pan. Place chicken breast into pan, crumb side down. Sauté without moving breast, about 4 minutes. Turn breast over and sear 2 minutes. Place in 400° oven for 5 minutes.

In a saucepan, bring heavy cream to boil and whisk in remaining mustard. Reduce sauce for 3 minutes and season to taste.

Pool sauce on plate and set chicken breast in sauce. Tastes good with a savory rice.

Alan P. Stewart
Oak Ridge Country Club

Ricotta Pancakes

3	eggs
1	teaspoon baking powder
	pinch salt
¼	pound ricotta cheese
⅔	cup milk
½	cup flour
1	cap almond extract

Separate eggs, whip whites and set whites aside.

Mix all other ingredients thoroughly. Fold in whipped egg whites.

Bake on preheated griddle. Use a fork and spatula to turn.

Top with blueberries or fruit of your choice. Also excellent with maple or other syrups.

Tom Herbst
The Inn in Vermont

Sourdough Tuscan Bread

Yields 4 loaves

Starter: Make 3 days prior to use.

¾	cup water
1½	cups unbleached flour
1	teaspoon yeast

Bread:

5	cups warm water
	starter, use all
¼	cup salt
1	tablespoon yeast
1	cup fresh rosemary and basil, chopped
2	tablespoons ground black pepper
11½	cups unbleached all–purpose flour

Combine all ingredients in large bowl and knead until smooth and elastic. Let sit in refrigerator overnight.

Divide cold dough into four loaves. Knead lightly and roll into round loaves. Cover and let double in bulk. Sprinkle with flour, flip loaves over and dust again with flour. Slice tops of loaves.

Bake at 400° for 20 minutes and finish bread at 350° until done. Cool to room temperature.

Steve Howard
D'Amico Cucina

Breadcrumbs fried to a deep gold in olive oil are used as a substitute for Parmesan in many pasta dishes all over Italy.

Bocce Chicken

Serves 4

Potatoes:

4	Idaho baking potatoes
1	cup heavy cream
¼	cup butter
	juice of 2 lemons
	salt and freshly cracked black pepper to taste

Chicken:

4	6–ounce breasts of chicken, boned and skinned
¼	cup butter
	salt and pepper to taste

Vegetables:

2	cups vegetables to include; green beans, red peppers, yellow peppers, zucchini, carrots, asparagus and fresh spinach.
4	tablespoons butter
1	cup chicken stock
3	tablespoons fresh herbs to include; parsley, rosemary, basil and thyme.

Steam and peel potatoes. Run through food mill or mash, using cream, butter, lemon juice, salt and fresh cracked pepper. Set aside and keep warm.

In ovenproof pan, sauté chicken breasts in butter at medium heat for 1½ minute on one side. Transfer pan to 400° oven and finish for 7 to 8 minutes. Set aside and keep warm.

Julienne all vegetables. Sauté vegetables, except spinach, and fresh herbs in butter. As butter begins to bubble, add chicken stock and cook briefly to tender-crisp. Add spinach and remove from heat.

Place mashed potatoes in center of four plates. Add one breast of chicken to each and cover with ½ cup vegetables. Add 2 to 3 tablespoons of vegetable sauce to each plate and serve immediately.

Sally Witham
Bocce

Bigos (Hunter's Stew)

½	pound each of pork, beef, veal and lamb
	or
	any leftover meats
1	pound Polish sausage (kielbasa), cut in small pieces
1	quart sauerkraut
1	head cabbage
1	large onion, chopped
½	pound mushrooms, sautéed
¼	pound bacon
1	glass of wine, optional
	water or vegetable stock
	salt and pepper

Slice cabbage thinly, sprinkle with salt and let stand 1 hour. In the meantime, wash the sauerkraut and cook until tender. Press out the moisture from cabbage and add to sauerkraut.

Cut bacon and fry. Add sautéed onion and meat and fry until meat is slightly brown. Add water or vegetable stock and cook until meat is tender.

Add Polish sausage and cabbage mixture and simmer for several hours, until flavors blend.

Bigos improves with reheating.

Eleanore Zarnowiecki

Stewed Mushrooms

Serves 4

1	pound Portabello mushrooms
1	cup olive oil
¼	cup garlic cloves, whole and peeled
1	bunch herb stems
2	tablespoons balsamic or red wine vinegar
	salt and pepper

Brush mushrooms with olive oil and grill until lightly browned. Slice mushrooms into ¼ inch strips.

Heat remaining oil in sauce pan and add sliced mushrooms. Reduce heat. Add remaining oil, garlic, herbs, vinegar, salt and pepper and let stew until garlic is tender.

Larry D'Amico
D'Amico + Partners

Lamb and Vegetable Salad with Honey Aioli

Serves 10 to 12

Lamb:

2	pounds lamb meat, cut from leg or loin
½	cup olive oil
¼	cup mixed herbs
1	ounce red wine vinegar

Vegetables:

12–18	medium red potatoes, washed
2	cups carrot coins, lightly blanched
2	medium red onions, cut in ½–inch slices
½	cup olive oil
3	tablespoons lemon juice
¼	cup mixed herbs
	salt and pepper

Season lamb with olive oil, salt, pepper, vinegar and herbs.

Cut potatoes in half and combine in bowl with blanched carrots. Season with ¼ cup olive oil, salt and pepper. Roast at 350° for 12 to 15 minutes until cooked but firm. Remove from oven and let cool. Toss onion in same bowl to coat with oil. Grill onion until lightly charred and cooked. Let cool and cut in half.

Toss potatoes, carrots and onions in bowl and season with remaining olive oil, lemon juice, herbs, salt and pepper.

Grill lamb to medium rare. Let rest and slice.

Serve lamb with vegetables and *Honey Lemon Aioli.

Honey Lemon Aioli

Serves 8

2	eggs
1	tablespoon garlic, minced
1	cup extra virgin olive oil
1	tablespoon lemon juice
	salt to taste
	cayenne pepper to taste
1	tablespoon orange blossom honey

Combine egg yolks and garlic in food processor and blend. Leave processor running and add oil in slow steady stream. If aioli becomes too thick, thin with cold water. Aioli should be the consistency of mayonnaise.

Season with salt, lemon juice and cayenne.

Jay Sparks
Azur

Pork Tenderloin with Pommery Vegetable Sauce

Serves 4

½	small onion
1	small carrot
½	red pepper
½	celery stalk
3	garlic cloves
2	green onions, including stems
3	cups chicken stock
	pinch thyme
2-3	ounces heavy cream
1½-2	tablespoons Pommery or seeded mustard
	salt and white pepper to taste
	dash Tabasco
2	12-ounce pork tenderloins with silver skins removed, trimmed of fat

Preheat oven to 425°.

Combine all vegetables in saucepan. Add enough chicken stock to cover. Add pinch of thyme. Simmer until tender, about 15-20 minutes.

Place in blender in 2 batches. Add 1 to 1½ ounces cream to each batch. Thin with chicken stock, if necessary.

Strain into saucepan. Add mustard, salt, pepper and Tabasco. Season to taste. Reduce over low heat, if mixture is too thin.

Season pork with salt, pepper and thyme. Place in hot skillet, turning to sear all sides. Place in oven for 4 to 5 minutes, depending on size of tenderloins. Remove from oven and let stand for 2 minutes.

Slice tenderloins and place on top of sauce. Serve.

Tim Scott
Postrio

Pork, like chicken, gets most of its flavor from the seasonings around it. Each cuisine of the world does its own unique thing with this wonderfully adaptable meat.

Charleston Dining Room, 1785–1820
Gift of Louise H. and James F. Bell in memory of Sallie M. and James S. Bell

PAINTED BY CHRISTOPH-FERDINAND CARON
MANUFACTURED BY SÈVRES
Tea Service for Twelve, French, 1807–08
Gift of the Groves Foundation

PAUL DE LAMERIE

Wine Cistern, 1719–20

The James S. Bell Memorial Fund

JOHN SINGER SARGENT
The Birthday Party, 1858
The Ethel Morrison Van Derlip Fund and the John R. Van Derlip Fund

Parties & Celebrations

You'll have no scandal while you dine,
But honest talk and wholesome wine.

—Alfred Lord Tennyson

Picnic in the Park

Season

Spring • Summer • Fall

Color Scheme

Vibrant colors appropriate for season

Invitation

Fanny–pack with invitation wrapped in bandana

Concept & Special Touches

Cycle to picnic spot and spread out blankets.

Center small tablecloth on each blanket and set "table" with fresh bandanas for napkins and coordinated paper goods.

Create a centerpiece using bubble makers of assorted shapes, sizes and colors pressed into a cube of polystyrene secured to the inside of a painter's plastic bucket. After picnic, remove from bucket and fill with bubble foam. Have fun!

Remember to pack away the refuse for disposal at home.

Menu

Crudités
Assorted Pâtés
Biscuits & Crusty French Bread
Cheese Platter
Condiments
Lime Tarts
Poached Pears with Caramel Sauce

Poached Pears with Caramel Sauce

Pears:
1	cup water per pear
¼	cup sugar per pear
1	vanilla bean per 4 pears
1	Bosc pear per serving, peeled and cored

Caramel Sauce:
⅓	cup granulated sugar
1	cup light brown sugar
¼	cup pure maple syrup
¼	cup corn syrup
1	cup heavy whipping cream

crème fraîche
sugar and cinnamon mixture
fresh mint leaf

Add water, sugar and vanilla bean to saucepan and bring to a boil, stirring until sugar is dissolved. Reduce heat and add pears. Simmer until tender, but not soft, approximately 10 minutes.

Remove pears and pack in traveling plastic container; chill. Best made early on morning of picnic.

Mix caramel sauce ingredients together in heavy bottom saucepan. Cook over high heat until mixture reaches 220° on candy thermometer. Let cool 20 minutes and skim surface if necessary.

To serve, place pear upright on plate, drizzle with caramel sauce and add a dollop of crème fraîche; sprinkle all with mixture of equal portions of sugar and cinnamon, top with a fresh mint leaf.

Patriotic Holiday Party

Season

Memorial Day or Independence Day

Color Scheme

Red, White and Blue

Invitation

White star sized to fit 5½ x 7½ envelope. Handwrite text in red or blue.
Encourage guests to wear casual clothing and sport shoes.

Concept and Special Touches

Play capture the flag, followed by an all–American cookout. Determine teams in advance, then as guests arrive use body paints to mark each forehead or cheek with a star or bell. Review the rules and be prepared for the adults to be as enthusiastically competitive as the children! Have prizes for winners and consolation awards for the losers.

For the cookout, let everyone participate. Provide several grills and ample equipment for individual hamburger tenders.

Use flags for centerpieces and decorations. Red carnations, greens and flags combine beautifully to create a stunning centerpiece for the buffet table. Arrange red, white and blue cups and napkins on a buffet table along with help–yourself foods, keeping dessert on ice in coolers at the end of the buffet tables.

End with a parade for which guests don hats and play instruments (recorders and drums) provided by the hosts and march to a Sousa recording. Cameras are a must!

Menu

Crudités: Carrots, Cauliflower, Broccoli, Jicama
Outside–in Hamburgers
Condiments: Chopped Onions, Chopped Tomatoes, Mustards, Chili Sauce, Mayonnaise, Ketchup, Assorted
Pickles and Olives, Chopped Bacon Crisps
Homemade Sweet Potato Chips
Frozen Chocolate–covered Ice Cream Bars

Outside–in Hamburgers

½   pound lean ground beef per guest serving
1   ounce cheese: Roquefort, Cheddar or soft white cheese per guest serving
1   hamburger roll per guest serving

Divide ½ pound ground beef into two flat patties; place cheese in center of one patty and top with other patty. Press edges together. Grill on both sides until tester inserted draws melted cheese, approximately six minutes on each side over hot coals.

Remove and place in roll warmed on grill.

Sweet Potato Chips

sweet potatoes, not yams
flour
salt and pepper
nutmeg, freshly grated
olive and canola oil in ratio of 1 to 4 for frying

Peel sweet potatoes and plunge into bowl of cold water. Dry each potato. Cut with thin slicer blade of food processor.

Dredge in flour, salt, pepper and freshly grated nutmeg. Deep fry until light brown and crisp. Drain well, adding more salt or freshly grated nutmeg before serving. May be done ahead and reheated at 275° for about 15 minutes.

CHANGING OF THE GUARD: A RETIREMENT SEND–OFF

Season

Your choice

Color Scheme

Coral and Aquamarine

Invitation

White card bordered in coral or aquamarine; print text in opposite color.

Concept and Special Touches:

Dress round tables in over–sized white cloths turned under and puffed to create a soft, elegant look; overlay with eight coral squares, allowing points of square to drop gracefully.

Tie deep coral napkins with aquamarine star vine. Use clear crystal plates and glasses.

Create centerpieces using 12–inch rocking or Adirondack chairs as a focal point. Place a miniature basket of asparagus fern on each chair seat; use glue gun to secure to each chair three coral–hued Gerbera daisies in water vials; cover mechanics with greens. Encircle the chair with greens and miniature objects that reflect the honored guest's interests. For a final touch, insert a slender coral mini–taper into each miniature basket.

Menu

Cheese Soufflé with Fresh Seafood Sauce
Green Salad with Fresh Raspberries, Toasted Walnuts and Raspberry Vinaigrette
Veal Medallions with Ginger Sauce
Green Asparagus Garnished with Red and Yellow Pepper and Topped with Lemon Zest
New Potatoes with Sour Cream and Caviar
Lime Mousse served in a Chocolate Cup
Champagne with Dessert

Veal Medallions in Ginger Sauce

Serves 6

6	medallions of veal
3	tablespoons butter
1½	tablespoons flour
2	large oranges
¼	cup stock
1½	tablespoons brandy
1	teaspoon ginger, freshly grated
6	thin slices ginger in syrup
	salt and pepper
	parsley and chives, chopped

Gently sauté medallions in butter until lightly browned; remove to platter and keep warm.

Stir flour into butter; add grated rind of one orange. Slowly stir in juice of one orange over low heat. Add stock, brandy and fresh ginger, stirring constantly. Add salt and pepper to taste and bring to a boil.

Peel and slice second orange. Heat slices in sauce for 3 minutes; remove. Return veal to pan and cook over medium heat for 5 minutes; remove.

Arrange one medallion on each plate; top with orange slice, chopped parsley, chives and ginger slice and drizzle sauce over all.

Lime Mousse

Serves 8

8	tablespoons sweet butter or margarine
5	eggs
1	cup granulated sugar
¾	cup fresh lime juice
	zest of 6 limes, grated
2	cups heavy cream

Melt butter in double boiler over simmering water.

Beat eggs and sugar until light and foamy. Add to melted butter. Cook, stirring constantly until it becomes custard–like, about 8 to 10 minutes.

Remove from heat, stir in lime juice and zest. Cool to room temperature.

Using an electric beater, whip cream until very, very stiff. Stir lime custard into whipped cream. Pour into 8 individual dishes, bowls or chocolate cups.

December Holiday Apron Exchange

Season

Christmas and Hanukkah

Color Scheme

Blues, Whites, Reds and Greens

Invitation

Handwrite or imprint text on recipe card and tie with ribbon to a cookie cutter. Add a blank recipe card. Wrap all in colored tissue and place in a padded envelope, addressed for mailing.

Concept and Special Touches

Invite friends for coffee 9:30–11:00 a.m. during the first week of December. On invitation ask each guest to bring a recipe written on the card provided, a gift–wrapped apron and a beribboned cookie cutter.
As each guest arrives, ask her to place the cookie cutter on a Menorah or a dowel–rod tree to create the centerpiece.

Have a table designated for the wrapped aprons or use an unusual holder such as an antique cradle decorated with a bouquet of greens and holly.

Collect recipe cards in a pretty china or wicker basket. Play holiday music in the background; consider having a pianist, perhaps one of the guests, lead informal holiday singing.

Draw numbers to establish order for guests to approach the apron cache to select a package. Open immediately and wear the delightful new apron.

As guests leave, remind them to select a new cookie cutter from the centerpiece and a recipe. Have pretty holiday bags ready at the door for each guest's gifts.

Menu

Cranberry and Date Breads
Scottish Scones
Strawberry, Lingonberry and Chutney Cream Cheese Spreads
Grilled Fruit Kabobs
Coffee and Mulled Cider
Cinnamon Sticks for Coffee and Cider

Scottish Scones

1	cup all–purpose flour
⅛	scant teaspoon baking soda
⅛	scant teaspoon salt
2	tablespoons sugar
⅔	cup buttermilk
1	large egg, lightly beaten
2	teaspoons sweet butter, melted
⅓	cup currants
1	tablespoon brown sugar
1	tablespoon butter

Preheat griddle and melt butter to coat.

Sift together flour, baking soda and salt. Stir in sugar. Stir in 2 teaspoons butter, buttermilk and egg, using a wooden spoon. Fold in currants.

Drop tablespoonsful of batter onto hot griddle. Cook until bubbling and undersides are golden brown. Turn over to cook other side to golden brown. Remove from griddle and keep warm until all scones are cooked.

Serve warm with clotted cream and preserves.

Grilled Fruit Kabobs

Macerate fruit for 1 to 3 hours in equal quantities of apricot juice and pineapple juice.

Alternate fruits of your choice on 6 to 8–inch wooden skewers: perhaps pineapple, mango and orange.

Remove skewers to broiler pan or grill, sprinkle with light brown sugar and broil or grill for 3 minutes, then turn skewer, sprinkle with sugar and broil or grill for additional 3 minutes.

Hawaiian Birthday Party for Six–Year–Olds

Season

Summer

Color Scheme

Any combination of bright colors such as yellow, orange and lime green

Invitation

Have your about–to–be six–year–old help cut out pre–traced pineapple shapes. Use bright, fine–line markers to write text. Add a note to encourage guests to wear hot colors: neon pink, purple and orange.

Concept and Special Touches

In preparation for the party, visit a craft shop to find materials to create leis; for example, string bright beads and artificial flowers on neon shoe laces and give one to each child. Also, consider grasses that could be tied onto a ribbon during the party to make a grass skirt or tie bright kerchiefs around cowboy hats for Hawaiian cowboys (paniola).

Have Hawaiian music playing as the children arrive and use it at game time for musical chairs. Invite a dance instructor to teach the hula.

Dress the table in a bright cloth and use napkins of varied colors. The centerpiece might be a plaster volcano, using dry ice to create an illusion.

Guests might each receive a small book about volcanoes or a story about a volcano might be read after serving birthday cake.

Finally, before going home, fish for prizes related to Hawaii: small surfboards, floral print bathing suits, miniature outrigger canoes, ukuleles.

Menu

Hawaiian Chicken
Pineapple and Orange Sorbet Balls on Pineapple Rings
Haupia (Coconut Pudding)
Palm–Tree Angel Food Cake with Butter Cream Frosting

Hawaiian Chicken

4	chicken breasts, skinned, boned and cubed
4	tablespoons soy sauce
2	tablespoons rice wine vinegar
½	teaspoon sugar
¼	cup unsalted butter
½	teaspoon fresh ginger, grated
1¼	cups chicken stock
4	green onions, sliced
1	tablespoon brown sugar
1½	tablespoons cornstarch
1½	tablespoons cold water

Combine soy sauce, vinegar and sugar. Marinate chicken 30 minutes.

Melt butter in wok; add ginger. Add chicken and sauté until golden brown. Add marinade, stock and onions. Cook over low heat for 15 minutes.

Combine brown sugar, cornstarch and water. Add to chicken mixture, stirring constantly, until mixture thickens.

May be served as is or over rice, Chinese noodles or in a blanched green pepper cup.

Haupia (Coconut Pudding)

3	tablespoons cornstarch
3	tablespoons sugar
⅛	teaspoon salt
2	cups coconut milk, divided
	ti leaves

Combine dry ingredients. Add ½ cup coconut milk; blend to smooth paste.

Heat remaining milk on low. Slowly add cornstarch mixture, stirring constantly; cook until smooth and thickened. Pour into shallow pan and let cool until firm.

Cut in small squares and serve on a ti leaf.

SEAFARING SCAVENGER HUNT

Season

August

Color Scheme

Marine Blue and White

Invitation

Tie printed invitations to plastic children's boats and deliver in marine blue bags.

Concept and Special Touches

Four to six boats with four crew each gather at a designated point on the lake.

Provide children's sandpails in bright colors for each boat and distribute scavenger hunt lists to each crew. Set time to reconvene, about one hour, on hosts' patio for prizes and dinner. Serve seafaring punch to launch the hunt.

Create centerpieces using asparagus ferns (to resemble seaweed) in glass bowls or arranged with driftwood in sandpails and treasures, such as: gold–foil covered coin–shaped chocolates, beading tied into necklaces and faux–gem rings.

Miniature boats hold place cards. Tie red napkins with white ship's line on marine blue tablecloths. Set table with blue spatterware for dinner service.

Menu

Rumrunners
Rusty Nails
Salty Dogs
Buccaneer Swordfish with Red Pepper Hollandaise
Renegade Rice Salad
Carrots Marguerite
Pirate's Pleasure Chocolate Cake

Renegade Rice Salad

Serves 16

3	cups long–grain rice
2	teaspoons salt, divided
3	teaspoons curry powder, divided
4½	tablespoons white wine vinegar
½	cup vegetable oil
1	cup golden raisins
1	large cantaloupe, seeded and cut into ½–inch pieces
1½	cups plain low fat yogurt
⅓	cup Major Grey's chutney
½	cup unsalted roasted peanuts

In a large kettle bring 5 quarts water to a boil, stir in rice and salt and stir until water returns to a boil. Boil 12 minutes. Drain rice in large strainer and rinse. Set the strainer over a large kettle of simmering water and steam rice covered with a kitchen towel and lid. Steam 20 minutes until rice is fluffy and dry. Place rice in very large bowl and cool to lukewarm.

In a small bowl whisk together the salt, 2 teaspoons curry powder, vinegar and oil. Add this vinaigrette to the rice and mix well. Stir in the raisins and melon.

In a blender, blend yogurt, chutney and 1 teaspoon curry powder until smooth. Pour dressing over rice mixture and toss salad well. Chill, covered, for 1 hour.

Sprinkle salad with peanuts and serve.

Salad can be made two days ahead and kept covered and chilled.

Carrots Marguerite

Serves 4

¼	cup butter or margarine
3	green onions (white part only), finely minced
1	pound carrots, shredded
3	tablespoons honey
½	teaspoon dried thyme leaves, crushed
¼	teaspoon salt
	dash pepper, freshly ground

Heat butter in large skillet over low heat. Sauté onions for a few minutes until soft and golden. Stir in carrots, honey, thyme, salt and pepper until carrots are coated. Cover and cook 3 minutes.

Serve immediately.

SOCK HOP

Season

Your choice

Color Scheme

Hot Pink and Black

Invitation

Hot pink bordered white card stock imprinted in black and affixed to 50's record, real or simulated.
Encourage costumes.

Concept and Special Touches

Dress 30–inch cabaret tables in black and white check or plaid tablecloths to the floor. Surround tables with black or white enameled chairs.

Create centerpieces by placing quart jars of hot pink long stemmed roses and greens inside shiny hot pink gift bags. Tie two hot pink and one black helium–filled balloons to each jar neck, allowing hot pink ribbons to extend almost to the ceiling. Vary heights of balloons, but avoid blocking sight lines. Black or white votive candles in clear glass holders complete the arrangement.

Play music from the 50's provided by a juke box or a disc jockey. Have ample room for dancing . . . . in socks, of course. Shoes have been removed and left at door upon arrival.

Activities might include a dance contest, musical chairs and the celebrity guessing game. The latter requires advance assignment of celebrity names to guests; names are written on self–adhesive name tags and placed on each guest's back as he or she arrives. Guests then ask questions of one another to determine who they are representing. That accomplished, the name tag is placed in the front of the person's garment.

Prizes may be awarded in keeping with the theme: socks, a tape or CD of 50's music, soda glasses.

Menu

Cherry Cokes & Root Beer Floats
Bowls of Popcorn & Tootsie Rolls
California Burgers
Potato Salad Exceptionale
Strawberry Gelatin & Fruit Cocktail Molds
Baked Alaska

Baked Alaska

1	quart peppermint ice cream, softened
1	9–inch round chocolate layer cake
6	egg whites (large eggs)
1½	teaspoons vanilla
¾	teaspoon cream of tartar
½	cup sugar

Line cookie sheet or baking pan with foil. Place cake on foil. Gently work ice cream out of container and onto cake. With flat, broad knife smooth ice cream over cake to cover surface, creating mounded shape. Wrap with cling film and freeze until firm.

Approximately 15 minutes before serving make meringue: beat together egg whites, vanilla and cream of tartar until soft peak stage; gradually add sugar and beat until stiff peak stage.

Remove cake from freezer and swirl meringue over cake to cover all. Bake in center of preheated 500° oven for 3 to 5 minutes. Watch carefully to avoid burning. Meringue should be golden and ice cream firm enough to slice.

Potato Salad Exceptionale

4	pounds red potatoes, cooked with skin on and chilled
6	hard boiled eggs, chopped
1	cup celery, diced
½	cup yellow onion, diced
2	cups mayonnaise
1	cup buttermilk
2	tablespoons salt
1	tablespoon white pepper
2	tablespoons American mustard

Mix together potatoes, eggs, celery and onions.

Combine mayonnaise, buttermilk, salt, white pepper and American mustard. Mix well. Toss with potato mixture.

Chill for two hours.

Musik in Garten: A German Celebration

Season

Spring

Color Scheme

Lilac and Teal

Invitation

White cards bordered in lilac; text printed in teal; or use invitations
with a green grape vine border and print in purple.

Concept and Special Touches

Use round tables of six, eight or ten and dress in a balanced mixture of lilac, teal and purple.

Create a circle of grapevine with tendrils and arrange fresh green and purple grapes on and around it. Add oak leaves to the arrangement if the season permits without damage to the trees. Plan a 36–inch lilac taper held in a crystal candlestick in the circle of grapevine. Add a few more leaves and grapes to the base of the candlestick.

Tie napkins of lilac, teal and purple with lilac French ribbon and place napkins on tables so that napkins and cloths are not the same color.

If possible, provide entertainment: perhaps a quartet playing only German composers or a group of dancers who would welcome your guests to join them in a dance around a Maypole.

Menu

Imported Cheeses and Game Pâté with Black Bread
Mixed Green Salad with Dried Fruits and Berries
Hunter Chicken with Braised Vegetables
Miniature Wiener Schnitzel with Lemon and Herbs
Fresh Peasant Breads and Yeast Breads
Black Forest Torte
Poppyseed Strudel
Lemon Tarts
Kopenhagener Schnecken (Puff Pastry with Sugar and Raisins)
Dark Coffee served with Whipped Cream and Chocolate Curls

Hunter Chicken

Serves 4

1	3½ pound chicken, quartered
1	cup tomatoes, diced
¼	cup parsnips, diced
1	cup carrots, diced
1	cup turnips, diced
1	cup potatoes, diced
2	tablespoons garlic, minced
8	ounces chicken stock
4	ounces veal demi
2	tablespoons fresh rosemary, chopped
	salt and pepper
¼	cup olive oil

Brown chicken in olive oil, using a heavy sauté pan. When chicken is cooked ⅔ of the way, add all the vegetables and garlic. Cook until garlic starts to brown, then add the chicken stock, veal demi and rosemary. Cook until chicken is fully done and the stocks have a brown sauce consistency.

Place the chicken in the center of each plate and spoon the vegetable sauce mixture over it. Serve hot.

Poppyseed Strudel

Filling:

1	cup black poppy seeds
1	cup milk
2	tablespoons butter, melted
5	tablespoons honey
½	cup almonds, chopped
	rind of ½ lemon, grated
1	tablespoon citron, chopped
½	cup raisins
½	cup sugar
1	tart apple, finely chopped

strudel dough
butter, melted

Mix together filling ingredients. Using basic strudel dough, lay on flat, floured surface, brush with melted butter and spread with filling. Roll up, place on baking pan.

Bake at 350° for 45 minutes.

Grandmother's Tea Party

Season

Your choice

Color Scheme

White

Invitation

Spur–of–the–moment telephone call extending invitation to children, their dolls and bears; encourage pretty dresses, hats and gloves.

Concept and Special Touches

Set tea table with beautifully pressed best white linens and lace. Use demi–tasse cups and saucers and coffee–sized spoons or child–sized tea cups and saucers. Use miniature silver or china tea service, if available.

Decorated sugar cubes are a pleasing touch: children love to experiment with sugar tongs.

Provide enough chairs for each guest and her entourage.

Place a beloved teddy bear or doll with a freshened dress in the center of the table and arrange a bouquet of flowers with ribbon streamers in the bear's or doll's arms.

Menu

Heart–shaped Egg Salad Sandwiches
Cucumber Finger Sandwiches
Bishop's Bread
Nan's Thimble Cookies
Miniature Lemon Tarts
Orange Spiced Herbal Tea in warm weather
Hot Cocoa in cold weather

Nan's Thimble Cookies

½	cup margarine
¼	cup sugar
1	egg, separated
½	teaspoon vanilla
2	tablespoons evaporated milk
1	teaspoon lemon rind, grated
1	teaspoon orange rind, grated
1¼	cups sifted flour
¾	cup finely chopped nuts
14	glazed cherries, halved

Cream margarine and sugar. Combine egg yolk, vanilla, milk and grated rinds. Stir into creamed margarine and sugar; beat well. Add flour and mix thoroughly. Chill.

Shape into teaspoon–sized rounds and partially flatten. Dip into slightly beaten egg white. Dip one flat surface into nuts, then using thimble create depression and place cherry half in it.

Bake on greased cookie sheet for 20 minutes in preheated 325° oven.

Arrange in silver basket with linen doily overhanging rim.

Mother's Miniature Lemon Tarts

½	cup lemon juice
1½	teaspoons lemon rind or zest, grated
1½	cups sweetened condensed milk
3	eggs, separated
¼	teaspoon cream of tartar
4	tablespoons sugar
12	miniature sweet pastry tart shells

Combine lemon juice and rind; gradually add milk. Stir in egg yolks until well blended. Chill overnight.

One hour before teatime, fill pastry shells with lemon mixture and make meringue: beat egg whites and cream of tartar to soft peak stage; gradually add sugar and beat to firm peak stage.

Put dollop of meringue on each tart and bake for 2 to 3 minutes in preheated 500° oven.

Remove tarts from tart tins and arrange tarts on plate with lace doily.

Farmer's Market Breakfast for Eight

Season

May through October

Color Scheme

Green and white

Invitation

Handwritten card tucked in straw farmer's hat

Concept and Special Touches

This is great entertainment for a visiting family.

Arrange to meet at 7:00 a.m. at designated point in market, perhaps the office or other spot where coffee is available. Saturday offers the greatest variety, but Sunday is less crowded.

Let the season and offerings inspire an ad hoc menu.

Hand a beribboned basket and menu assignment to each two guests; scramble partners for fun. Agree to reconvene at 7:45 a.m. to head for home.

Have the kitchen ready and the table set, using green and white plaid napkins and green placemats. Provide space in the refrigerator for guests' purchases.

Supplies to have at hand include freshly squeezed orange juice, flavorful coffee, butter, oil, broth for soup, spices and aprons.

Menu

Fruits for a starter
Ingredients for a frittata
Greens and herbs for a salad
Ingredients for a light soup
On your way home, swing by your favorite croissant purveyor.
Flowers for the table

Acknowledgments

Seven decades after its modest beginnings, the Friends of the Institute remains dedicated to "broadening the influence of the museum in the community."

Committee

President of the Friends
Joan Hutton

Honorary Chairperson
Patricia Jaffray

Chairperson
Mary Taylor

Secretary
Kathie Harder

Treasurer
Frances Tobian

Recipe Collection
Norma Phelps

Recipe Testing
Judy Pierpont

Additional Copy
Mary Bowman
Laurel Keitel

Editors
Nancy Aldrich
Sharon Baumgartner
Gloria Smith

Layout Editors
Nancy Aldrich
Kathie Harder
Gloria Smith

Marketing
Bette Englund
Kristi Gray

Advisory Committee
Jack Farrell
Sara Monick
Dode Wheaton
Sue Zelickson

Friends Coordinator
Carol Lierle

Acknowledgments

Professional Contributors

Dr. Evan Maurer, Director
S. Timothy Fiske, Associate Director
Ruth Dean
Robert Jacobsen
Susan Jones
Mark Jung
Carol Lierle
Sandra Lipschultz
Jill McTaggert
Catherine Parker
Elisabeth Sövic
Mathew Welch
Curatorial Staff
The Minneapolis Institute of Arts

Vickie Abrahamson
Icon Corporation

J. Benjamin Ahrens
Maslon, Edelman, Borman & Brand

Tim Anderson
Goodfellow's

Jack Anderberg
Diane Mead
Claudia Olson
Anderberg Lund Printing Company

Burt Cohen
MSP Communications

Eleanore Zarnowiecki
D'Amico Partners, Inc.

Rose Goehring
Neiman Marcus

Miranda Moss
Yamamoto/Moss

Pentair, Inc.

Terry Ilse
Terese Lynch
Robin Schribman
Dory Skartvedt
Tad Ware & Company Inc.

Meg Colwell
*Viking Press,
A Banta Corporation Subsidiary*

Color Separations Furnished by:
*Color Response,
A Banta Corporation Subsidiary*

Title and copyright research done by:
*Thomson & Thomson
500 E Street. S.W.
Suite 970
Washington, D.C. 20024
(800) 356-8630*

Friends of the Friends

When Friends Cook wishes to acknowledge and thank all of those who contributed recipes, tested recipes, promoted the sales and in other ways supported the creation of this book. Their diligence and commitment has made When Friends Cook the quality publication that it is.

Credit goes to Val Seaberg, who thoughtfully named this book.

Kristine Aasheim	Barbara Bellows	Kay Carda
Chloe Ackman	Lorraine Benson	Anne Carrier
Kathy Adams	Marilee Bergerson	Barbara Carriger
Mary Adams	Nancy Bergerson	Theresa Carufel
Betsy Aldrich	Judy Bermel	Joanne Case
Mark Aldrich	Carolyn Berman	Kathy Churchill
Nancy Aldrich	Theresa Berman	Doris Clegg
Lucille Amis	Sharon Bigot	Olivia Coan
Evie Anderson	Ann Birt	Rusty Cohen
Janice Anderson	Alexandra Boardman	Mary Collins
Marian Anderson	Donna Bonello	Denise Colon
Mary Sue Anderson	Sheila Bonsignore	Phyllis Colwell
Marion Andrus	Lorraine Born	Tyler Congdon
Margie Ankeny	Mary Bowman	Ella Crosby
Sally Anson	Carol Brooks	Ellie Crosby
Elizabeth Armstrong	Marney Brooks	Harriett Dayton
Margaret Arnar	Jean Buckley	Joan Dayton
Patrick Atherton	Barbara Budd	Ruth Dean
Jo Bailey	Kate Budd	Stephen Dean
Barbara Hannaford Bakewell	Polly Bullock	Lucy Denham
Gilda Banfield	Beachy Bunting	Alma Derauf
Nancy Bauer	Virginia Bureau	Janice Derrig
Sharon Baumgartner	Bobbie Burritt	Mary Desjardon
Mary Becker	Russ Bursch	Barbara Diamond
Diane Bellafronto	Carol Burton	Ann Dietrich

Jack Dietrich
Sonia Dobson
Beth Dooley
Julie Drake
Elizabeth Driscoll
Judy Driscoll
David Duff
Lucy Dunning
John Easley
Mary Easley
Catherine Ecklund
Jetabee Edman
Silas Edman
Bette Englund
Kay Erickson
Marion Errede
Anne Everett
Kathy Farley
Jack Farrell
Geren Fauth
Rosella Fefercorn
Bruce Field
Peggy Fink
Jim Fish
Carol Fiske
Dorothy Fobes
Lyn Foster
Margene Fox
Ellen Frank
Penny Freeman
Sharon Fuller
Jan Gaele
Marilyn Gamble

Mrs. David Gerrish
Paula Smith Gilmore
Rose Goehring
Anne Goldston, M.D.
Beverly Grace
Jeanne Grandy
Kristi Gray
Stanley Gregory
Jonathan Griebel
Rosemary Griggs
David Grose
Polly Grose
Alice Guiher
Norma Hanlon
Sally Hanser
Peggy Hanson
Kathie Harder
Roxanne Hardy
Claire Hartley
Lucy Hartwell
Ruth Hass
Sally Hauser
Sally Healey
Diane Heeter
Nancy Heeter
Arlene Helgeson
Marnie Hensel
Jan Hereid
Joanne Hitch
Sue Hodder
Bill Humphrey
Marge Humphrey
Marilyn Hunt

Lois Husbands
Joan Hutton
Polly Jackson
Susan Jacobsen
Patricia Jaffray
Betty Jewett
Arne Johnson
Esther Johnson
Helen Johnson
Mary D. Johnson
Rosie Johnson
Anne Winton Johnston
Jock Jones
Kathy Jones
Orlie Jones
Susan Jones
Jane Kaufman
Mary Keating
Laurel Keitel
Michele Keith
Mary Kell
Maggie Kelly
Heather King
Marilyn Kingman
Mary Kjell
Don Knutzen
Helen Knutzen
Donna Koelsch
Betty Koss
M. Pauline Krieger
Jean Krogness
Mary Kunz
Catharine Larson

Madrienne Larson	Patty McCullough	Steven Okey
Jennifer Layton	Suzanne McCune	Sue Olin
Martha Leonard	Judy McCuskey	Mary Olson
Margaret Leddick	Joyce H. McFarland	Tom Opem
Wilma Leland	Mary McGrath	Allegra Parker
Dorothy Levy	Jill McTaggert	Joan Parsons
Sara Lieberman	Paulette Mitchell	Suzanne Payne
Carol Lierle	Virginia Moertel	Cathy Peel
Maggie Lierle	Ann Moffitt	Rae Pesek
Peggy Lindborg	Margaret Molander	Julia Peterson
Gretchen Lindgren	Sara Monick	Katy Peterson
Patricia Lindgren	Kate Mooney	Nancy Peterson
Maris Logan	Melissa Moore	Margaret Pfohl
Jean Long	Sylvia Moore	Katharine Phelps
Elizabeth Longfellow	Mary Alice Mork	Norma Phelps
Teedee Ludwick	Bruce Morrow	Jonathon Pierpont
Denise Luke	Scott Bryan Moses	Judy Pierpont
Jacqueline Maas	Mary Mugg	Maxine Pierpont
Ann Mack	Jan Mulfinger	Scott Pierpont
Lucy Mack	Betty Murphy	Kitty Pillsbury
Gray Mackay	Pat Nasby	Nina Pillsbury
Sally MacMillan	Jacqueline Neilson	Sally Pillsbury
Terri MacPhail	Bea Nelson	Susan Platou
Nancy Madden	Edna Nelson	Becky Pohlad
Whitney Magee	Frances Nelson	Patricia Poore
Marion Mahoney	Jane Nelson	Stephanie Prudden
Janet Margolis	Lance Nelson	Gretchen Quie
Martha Mason	Pat Nelson	Ann Randall
Sally Mathieu	Judy Neumeier	Carol Raschke
Kathy Matthew	Shirley Nilsen	Mary Raymond
Lee Mauk	Orrell Nilsson	Ellie Reid
Barbara McBurney	Nancy Nolan	Mary Revello
Edie McClintock	Ellie Ogden	Jorie Richards

Patricia Ringer
Margaret Ringstrom
Sharon Ritchie
Mary Ritten
Ricki Roberts
Sue Roberts
Jo Robles
Gladys Rogers
M.E.G. Roy
Ann Rudd
Elizabeth Ruedy
Joel Rumme
Jo Ruth
Keith Rutten
Mary Ann Sahs
Edna Sanfilippo
Angela Sangster
Barbara Sarbach
Barbara Savage
Katharine Schooley
Nancy Schwalm
Carolyn Schwantes
Cynthia Scott
Tim Scott
Janet Seidenberg
Ben Shank
Kitty Shen
Preena Sheps
Margot Siegel
Anne Simonson
Susan Siragusa
Gloria Smith
Phil Smith

Neil Sontag
Barbara Souther
Elizabeth Spencer
Carol Stampfli
Mary Steeber
Peggy Steiner
Ruth Bovey Stevens
Shawn Stokes
Charles Stone
Dick Strand
Joan Strand
Michael Studor
Jan Sundberg
Cynthia Sutter
David Swanson
Elaine Swanson
Voni Swenson
Helen Taylor
Jack Taylor
Mary Taylor
Katharine Tearse
Marian Thiele
Barbara Tiede
Frances Tobian
Louis Tobian
Joanne Topp
Linda Towle
Eleanor Trnka
Carol Truesdell
Mary Tuttle
Martha Twigs
Pat Van Valkenburg
Teresa Vickery

Jorgen Viltoft
Mildred Visgar
Ann Warner
Mrs. John Watling, Jr.
Ruth Weed
Sarah Weld
Ellen Wells
Jane West
Pat West
Dorothy Westmoreland
Teresa Whaley
Jane White
Virginia White
Shirley Whitlock
Helen Whitney
Marian Williams
Jenny Wilson
Jeannine Winkelman
Ronnie Winsor
Angie Woodhouse
Joan Wyer
Elli Zarnowiecki
Betty Zats
Sue Zelickson
Ann Zelle
Elizabeth Zempel

All of our friends at Viking!

If we have failed to include anyone who has made a contribution, please accept our sincere apologies.

Index

INDEX

* indicates that recipe is in this book.
Please refer to index.

—Notes—